P9-CDU-860

Teach Me Mommy
A Preschool Learning Guide

3rd Edition

By Jill W. Dunford
Illustrated by Heather D. Nemelka

GLOUCESTER CRESCENT PUBLISHING
SNELLVILLE, GA USA

Copyright @ 2000 Jill W. Dunford. Printed in the United States of America. All rights reserved. No part of this work may be reproduced or transmitted in any form of by any means, electronic or mechanical, including photocopying and recording, or by any information storage or retrieval system, without permission in writing from the publisher except by a reviewer who may quote brief passages in a review. Published by Gloucester Crescent International.
Internet: www.teachmemommy.com

Library of Congress Cataloging in Publication Data

Dunford, Jill
    Teach Me Mommy

    Includes bibliographies
    Includes index
    1. Education. Preschool - Curricula - Handbooks, manuals, etc. 2. Creative activities and seat work - Handbooks, manuals, etc. 3. Play groups - Handbooks, manuals, etc. 4. Domestic Education - Handbooks, manuals, etc. 5. Children's literature - Bibliography. I. Title.

    Print Version ISBN 0-931151-01-5; Electronic Version ISBN 0-931151-02-03
    (previously published ISBN 0-931151-01-5, 0-9311151-00-7, 0-89879-187-1
    LB1140.444.D.85   1985   649:51 85-11926)

To
Matthew,
Heather,
Clayton,
Adam,
Benjamin,
Bryan,
and Brittany
without whom none of this
would ever have come about!

And to my grandchildren
who will benefit
from what their parents
have learned...

ACKNOWLEDGMENTS

It has been more than twenty years since my magazine article about our home nursery school was published. There have been so many friends and acquaintances who have faithfully encouraged me to put our program down on paper for others. Thanks should go especially to my own children, and my daughter-in-law, Tana.

Of course, the delightful illustrations in this new, third edition would not have been possible without the talents of my daughter, Heather Dunford Nemelka. My sons, Adam and Bryan, helped format it all and helped with the full size pattern pages. And now my son Matt is putting it all on the Web at www.teachmemommy.com.

My parents, Clarence and Nancy Wonnacott, have my never ending thanks for always encouraging me to do my best and to go beyond myself. The time that they spent teaching and reading to me has carried over to the raising of my own children.

Most of all, my deepest gratitude goes to my husband, Rob, for having the faith in me and for helping me to get my ideas from file folders to book form. He has been my strongest support and help.

CONTENTS

CHAPTER 1
WHY HAVE A HOME NURSERY SCHOOL?

Nearly twenty-six years ago when our oldest son, Matthew, was four, I explored the various nursery schools to which we might send him. The choice was based on the school's reputation, cost, the distance from our home, and other factors. Eventually, we narrowed our choice down to two.

The first was a co-op group that was inexpensive, but the mothers were required to help a certain amount of time each month. With two other pre-schoolers, I would have had to find a baby-sitter for them on those days, which was an impossibility, both from a cost and a time standpoint.

The second school required no time on my part, and, though quite expensive, it seemed the best choice with my time limitations.

After several weeks, however, I found my son becoming increasingly unhappy. He enjoyed school, but he would return home tense and demanding. In addition, he acquired some new words I didn't like. I felt that something was going wrong somewhere.

It was at this time that my husband and I sat down to analyze exactly what our purpose was in sending Matthew to preschool. We knew we wanted him to gain social skills before he started kindergarten and become familiar with a school learning structure. Furthermore, we wanted to help him broaden his horizons and become acquainted with the world in which he lived. As we talked about what we wanted for him, an idea began to form—why couldn't we have our own nursery school just for our children? The more we thought about it, the better the idea sounded.

We talked with several preschool experts in both public and private schools. One of these "experts" said she personally would like to see all families do what we were considering. She felt that the nurturing time between a mother and child during the preschool years was much more important than the associations he could be making with other children.

With this kind of encouragement, I read numerous books and periodicals on the subject. I studied the curriculum used in the child development preschool at a nearby state university. I talked to teachers and visited a number of preschools. Then, on a trial-and-error basis, I developed our program. As our children grew, their needs and situations varied. Nursery school time was always adapted to each child's needs and his/her interest span.

When my youngest child turned five, she was one week behind the cutoff for kindergarten. So that year, I put her into a mother's morning-out program once a week besides *Teach Me Mommy*, so she could begin to associate with other children in a learning situation. Does that surprise you to learn that? No, remember that my philosophy about pre-schooling (and it should be yours too) is that your program should meet the needs of **your** child. That doesn't mean that you send him off to a commercial nursery school at the age of two. A balance should be made which is in the best interests of each of your children. Keep them with you as long as possible!

1

FREQUENTLY ASKED QUESTIONS

How old should a child be to begin home preschool?
Three years old, or two years before the child will begin school, is a good time to start. That doesn't mean you shouldn't spend activity time with younger children. Reading to children should start from the time that they are babies, and there should always be time spent in finger plays, painting, playing with play dough, etc. However, by age three, most children have a long enough attention span to appreciate and enjoy a more structured learning situation.

We live in an area with very few children for my son to play with. Don't I need to send him to a preschool, so he can have interaction with other children before he begins kindergarten?
The answer to this depends upon how old the child is. If he is three or under, I would say, "No!" He can become just as autonomous on his own at this time alone with you than with others. This can be the time to build his skills—listening, drawing, thinking, counting—then he will have the self-confidence he needs when he is with other children more. If he will be starting school in a year, short periods of time (2–3 hours) two or three times a week are a good way to introduce him to situations involving other children and social experiences. You could contact other mothers and have a play group where the children would rotate homes and spend a morning or two a week together.

I am a working parent but would like to spend some quality time with my child every day. How can I best utilize your book?
The units and days are organized so that you can select how many activities you use and how many books you read. The preparation time is minimal. The book is set up to coincide with the school year with lesson plans for three days each week. If you are not going to be able to spend that much time, you may want to eliminate a chapter from time to time, to coordinate your lessons with the seasons. I know a divorced father who has his preschooler on the weekend. He uses **Teach Me Mommy** to have activities planned when he sees his daughter.

I have three preschoolers. How can Teach Me Mommy work for me?
I always tried to time our nursery school activities so that the baby was down for a nap. When I have had younger children "attending" too, their attention span has naturally not been as long, so I also tried to provide them with other toys to amuse themselves at the same time.

Won't a child be poorly adjusted in kindergarten if he hasn't attended a commercial preschool program?
Our children have had no problems adjusting to school and leaving home for that time each day. Rather, since they had adjusted to learning situations in our home, they were eager and willing to start kindergarten. Their teachers have frequently commented that they are confident and knowledgeable in so many subjects. They have interaction with other children at church and in our neighborhood, so it has not been hard for them to make the adjustments to being with other children in school.

The results of research conducted internationally supports my own experience. In an excellent review of studies undertaken in 13 countries to determine results of various types and settings of preschool instruction, the first two of five generalizations that emerge are these:

- "There is *widespread evidence* that participating in a *preschool program* promotes cognitive development in the short term and *prepares children to succeed in school.*
- "There is *no strong or consistent evidence* that the *form* of the preschool experience (pedagogic approach, daily schedule, or setting [i.e., home preschool vs. commercial preschool]) influences long-term outcomes for children."

The reviewer goes on to cite a massive study in the U.K.: "Comparisons among children who attended play groups, private or public nursery schools, or no preschool at all showed that *experience in any preschool* (including play groups) contributed to cognitive development and school achievement throughout the period studied. Disadvantaged children gained slightly more from attending preschool than did more advantaged children. Contrary to the researchers' expectations, preschool experience did not affect aspects of children's socioemotional development, such as self-concept, skill in getting along with other children, or their ability to apply themselves to schoolwork."

The researchers concluded that "*preschool experience per se had more influence* on children's subsequent development than the *type* of preschool attended. 'Provided the child receives proper care, has interesting activities and other children to play with (which are common elements in the majority of preschool institutions), *the actual type of preschool experience matters very little.*'" (Italics mine. Source: *Early Childhood Programs in Other Nations: Goals and Outcomes*, Sarane Spence Boocock Ph.D., professor of sociology at the Graduate School of Education at Rutgers University, 1995. Available online at: http://www.futureofchildren.org/lto/05_lto.htm)

Of course, every child is different and so I say again, **meet your child's needs**.

I don't have a lot of free time in my day. Can I really do preschool teaching successfully?
If you're like most (68%) of the mothers in America with children at home, you are in the labor force. There is a definite amount of time involved in preparation and organization for each day's study. Hopefully, this manual will make it easier for you. Even if one doesn't have to work, we all spend time each week doing housework, cooking meals, preparing for church, and volunteering in the community, etc. Isn't time spent with our children well worth it? After the initial preparation and material gathering, the work is minimal.

I run a preschool. Your ideas are excellent. Can I adapt them?
Certainly. Sometimes the phraseology needs to be changed. In units such as Chapter 4, Day 1, Who is in My Family?, you may want to have each child bring a picture of his/her whole family to share. You can put the pictures on a bulletin board for the week. If you have children of other nationalities or ethnic groups, their parents could be good resources for the December holiday chapter.

I have found that I need to go back to work. How can I choose a nursery school or day care center for my preschooler?
That is a very important but sometimes difficult question to answer. Here are some criteria you might want to use:

- Ask other mothers about different schools and what they liked or disliked about each. Of course, everyone's opinion is different, but it should help you narrow down the field.
- Talk to the school director and determine his or her philosophy about preschool education. Some may put a lot of emphasis on play, while others may emphasize intense learning. Only you can determine what approach you want to see used with your child.
- Visit the school and sit in a classroom to get a feel for the attitudes of the teachers. This will tell you a lot about the atmosphere there. Plan on spending at least 30 minutes.
- Check on the ratio of children to teacher. Eight or ten to one is ideal. If there is a large class with only one teacher and no assistants, you can be sure that there will be neglect for many (even though the teacher wants to meet everyone's needs).
- Determine what kind of training and background the teacher has had. I was surprised to learn that many states have no requirements as to training and teacher competency when giving preschool licenses. A teacher doesn't need to have a college degree, but they should have had some education in preschool or young child instruction.

You still should try to have your own nurturing time with your child, however, whether he is in someone else's nursery school or not. The activities in this book will help you do this with a minimum of time and preparation.

Just out of curiosity, how did *your* children do in school, now that they are nearly all grown?
I have just one child at home now—Brittany, a senior in high school—so I think I can look back with some perspective. From the outset, my primary objective was not to have my children be accelerated beyond their peers. Instead, my primary objective was to *nurture* them by *spending time* with them and *strengthening the natural bonds* between mother and child. I hesitate to respond to your question for fear of appearing immodest, but I believe that **Teach Me Mommy** and the time I was able to spend with my children in this program contributed significantly to the fact that:

- all seven of our children were invited to be in gifted programs in their schools
- two were National Merit Finalists and two were Semi-Finalists
- three were presidents of the National Honor Society (an academic honors society for high school students)
- four were school newspaper editors
- six graduated, or will graduate, in the top 5% of their class
- two were finalists in Governor's Honors for the State of Georgia
- two were STAR students (highest SAT scores)
- they have so far earned nearly $100,000 in tax-free scholarships for college
- all benefited from taking Advanced-Placement courses which gave them college credit and saved them and us thousands more by testing out of many lower-level college courses

The last two points are important, because there was no way we could get all these kids through college on my husband's income alone! The older children are currently in graduate programs (medical and dental schools) or are married or both and the younger ones (except Brittany) are undergraduates or married or both. Again, academic achievement was not our primary objective. It was an unplanned yet happy result of the time we spent together.

Lest you be concerned that these children excelled only academically, we have had five Eagle Scouts, one Atlanta Football Club Scholar Athlete, three All-State Orchestra or All-State Chorus finalists, six student body or senior class officers and one Miss Teen Of Georgia, as well. There are many other things that go into raising successful children besides preschool. I believe, however, that the foundation laid in our **Teach Me Mommy** program gave them a significant head start. We feel extremely fortunate and grateful that each one continues to do well.

IN CONCLUSION

As I consider our home nursery program that began so many years ago, I have reached the following conclusions:

- It was a wonderful opportunity for me to spend quality, nurturing time with my children. I don't know a child who wouldn't rather spend time with his own mother playing, reading, and learning.
- When our baby was awake and our two-year old was restless, the ratio of teacher to child was still only one to three, which is much better than in any commercial nursery program.
- Nursery school has been a good opportunity for my older children to help prepare things for the little ones to use. They helped mount pictures and clip stories. Many times, the one in kindergarten told a story he had read or something he had done in school that I could use. On days when my older children were out of school because of snow, they have even been the teachers.
- I also have been able to control the material used to teach my children. My purpose in having a home nursery school was not to try to teach our children to read or count at a young age, but for them to look to their parents as a source of knowledge and understanding. I didn't pressure our children to develop more quickly than they were ready. However, I did teach our children skills such as the handling of scissors and the use of crayons, glue, and books. I also tried to help them have confidence in their ability to learn things and to understand what others will be teaching them in the future.

The most important thing is that you spend time with your children! The time that a parent has with a child before he starts school is so short. It is important that children have the loving attention of their parents as much as possible.

Once, after one of our children visited an excellent nursery school in a former community, he came home saying that he liked our nursery school better, because he could be with Mommy. That assured me that all the effort was worth it. There are few joys equal to teaching your children within the walls of your own home!

GETTING STARTED
EQUIPMENT
RESOURCE MATERIAL
TEACHING AIDS
P.S.

GETTING STARTED

This book contains the directions you will need to begin and develop your home preschool. The materials are geared to children from ages three to five, although many of the ideas can be used for an older child as well. **Remember to gear your activities to the skills of your child.** For example, a three-year-old will become frustrated if he is expected to be proficient with scissors, but a five-year-old can master that skill. Some of the crafts and many of the treats are prepared mainly by the adult, but the child can help as he is able. Don't pressure him to do things his young body is not ready for yet.

Begin by making a file folder or a large manila envelope for each subject you will be covering during the year (see **Table of Contents** for the subjects you will probably want to use). Then, begin to fill them with ideas you find. For example, I went through old magazines and catalogs to find pictures I could use. The public library is a rich resource for books on various subjects, including craft ideas that can be incorporated into various themes. Over the years, I've found new pictures and stories to add. Older children will bring home ideas from school that can be adapted to the younger one's learning. In addition, I looked through recipe books to find treats and surprises that could be used with some of the topics. As you go along, you'll find many new ideas and sources you will want to add.

Next, develop a simple plan for each day. Our "school" is set up for three days a week, for one and a half to two hours a day. If that is too much for you, begin with just twice a week. The important thing is that, barring emergencies, once you have set the time, stick with it! Schedule appointments or other activities for non-school days or times. Your children will quickly learn when you will be meeting and will need that order in their lives. Feel free to skip days or skip around so that the book resources will fit **your** situation and time schedule. If you work doing the week and are doing *Teach Me Mommy* on the weekend, compact the week into one day's activities and do that.

A blank weekly outline that I use is included at the end of this chapter. It's based on the format used in the various chapters in this book, but if this doesn't work for you, feel free to make up your own! By filling out the outline in advance, you can quickly see the things you'll need each week and what you need to plan for. An example follows:

SUBJECT: FAMILIES

	MONDAY:	WEDNESDAY:	FRIDAY:
INTRO.	DESCRIBE FAMILY MEMBERS —LET THEM GUESS WHO THEY ARE LOOK AT PICTURES OF FATHERS, MOTHERS, ETC.	SHOW PICTURE OF FATHER —WHAT DOES HE DO? —WHAT DO OTHER MEMBERS DO?	SHOW PICTURE OF GRANDPARENTS, TALK ABOUT THEM
BOOKS	ARE YOU MY MOTHER? WANTED... A BROTHER	JUST ME AND MY DAD TEN, NINE, EIGHT	GRANDMOTHER LUCY MARY JO'S GRANDMOTHER
FINGERPLAY, RECORD, SONG	FINGER FAMILY	/	MY GRANDMOTHER
ART WORK, CRAFT, PROJECTS	DO FAMILY MOBILE— WHITE POSTER BOARD, CRAYON, CLOTHES HANGER, THREAD	MAKE COUPONS FOR FAMILY MEMBERS — WHITE PAPER, CRAYONS (COPY COUPON PGS.)	DECORATE FRAME GET PHOTOS TO CHOOSE FROM, BUTTONS TO GLUE ON, CRAYONS
TREATS	MARSHMALLOW PEOPLE— MARSHMALLOWS, TOOTH-PICKS	MAKE A COOKIE FOR EACH FAMILY MEMBER FOR DINNER	GRANDMA'S GINGERSNAPS

Now let's discuss the steps used in these chapters. Most areas have an identifying picture so you can quickly locate what activity to move to next.

MATERIALS:

Each day has a list of materials needed. Having these items on hand will allow you to better present the information and concepts for the day. Most of the time, snacks are not individually listed because those are often more complex. However, when you fill out your work sheet, be sure and list what you need for the snack you have chosen.

PROJECTS:

Because there are several projects to choose from, you can decide which one you would like to do depending upon your time, resources, and child's age. You will only need the items listed next to that particular project.

INTRODUCTION:

Begin each day with some introduction time. This is when you acquaint your child with the day's material. Most of what you need to say is written out for you, but you will want to add your own thoughts. We spend from five minutes to half an hour on this, depending on the material and the attention span of the child.

The introductions in this book have been kept simple deliberately . If your child wants to know more, you can turn to an encyclopedia or other books to help him increase his knowledge and answer his questions. The National Geographic Society has published a number of books in its "Young Explorer" series that are marvelous resources for a number of lessons. Specific titles will appear in appropriate units. A catalog of the books available can be received by writing:

> National Geographic Society
> Books for Young Explorers Pub.
> P. O.. Box 2118
> Washington, DC. 20013-2118
> 1-800-447-0647

BOOKS:

Next, I read one or more books to reinforce what we learned in the introduction. I have included many we have liked and reread through the years. After studying the lessons, I try to find these books at the library several weeks in advance, so I can make adjustments and changes in the lesson if I need to. You will want to add to this bibliography as you find other books that your children enjoy. New books on each subject are published all the time, so feel free to choose what looks interesting to you.

We have also purchased many of our favorites, which are now well-loved and well-worn! The Golden Book Press, Inc. has published a wide variety of books that can be purchased at toy stores, discount stores or even supermarkets for under $2.00. These are nice, because they allow the child the opportunity to have his own books at a nominal cost.

I also want to mention a book that every parent should own. This is *The Read-Aloud Handbook* by Jim Trelease, Penguin Books. This national bestseller discusses how parents reading stories to their children is important in the mental and creative development of a child. It includes a large bibliography of books appropriate from preschool through teenage years.

FINGERPLAYS:

Many chapters have finger plays the child can act out. Some of these are combined with song melodies.

SONGS:

Simple melody lines of most of the songs appear in the Appendix, so you can play them on the piano or keyboard if you wish. There are also a number of fun songbooks for children that you might want to use. Two we enjoy are:

> *Children's Favorites*. A Walt Disney Story Tape with 25 familiar songs and words in a book and cassette tape. Available at toy or record stores.

> *Reader's Digest Children's Songbook*, The Reader's Digest Association, Inc., 1985. One of the best collections that I've seen of favorite modern songs, (such as Muppets and Sesame Street tunes, movie songs and cartoons,) nursery rhymes and many old favorites. It comes with an extra book with just the lyrics.

Children love music and sometimes need only a song to get them walking like elephants or "flying" like airplanes. You can also buy tapes and play them on a cassette player. Libraries have tapes which can be checked out. Feel free to get into the act and don't be inhibited. A child loves it when his parents act and play with him!!

PROJECTS AND ACTIVITIES:

Next comes activity time. I have provided several projects or activities to choose from for each day. Some require a lot of preparation or more help from the parent than others. Some involve a field trip. Choose what works best for your child or children and for your time. **Remember you don't need to do all the crafts listed—just pick one or maybe two.** For example, Chapter 3, Day 1, My Name and Age, you can choose to make a growth chart, a birthday cake card or name plaques. You don't need to do all three activities. The projects and activities you don't do can be saved for next year.

SNACKS:

In many lessons, I have suggested snacks that are appropriate for what you are studying. Choose one. You may also want to save these treats for the preschooler to share with the whole family at dinner time. You can make appropriate substitutions if salt or sugar intake is a problem. I also have found that just a glass of juice and a cracker is a nice way to end our time together. Some of the snack suggestions take some time, so you might want to do those as your project activity. If you don't have time to make homemade treats, purchased ones are just fine. Pre-made sugar cookie dough is available in the dairy section of your supermarket. Nice round cookies (such as Keebler Pecan Sandies® and many low fat brands now on the market) can be frosted to give to family members in Chapter 4, Families, decorated to look like pumpkins in Chapter 8, Halloween, or frosted pink with candy hearts for Chapter 16, Valentines.

EQUIPMENT:

Here are some items I use a lot. Most of the items are available at an office supply, school supply, fabric, or craft store. Make sure you have your supplies in advance so you aren't hunting for a pair of scissors while your child is waiting impatiently. An empty apple box will hold just about everything listed here except the newsprint paper.

Brown paper bags: both lunch and grocery bags are used for a number of crafts.

Butcher or newsprint paper: available from school supply stores, but many newspapers will let you have the ends of rolls for free. This is good where large sheets of paper are needed to draw the child's outlines or to cover cardboard boxes.

Cardboard: my husband saves the backs of pads of paper from work to serve as a backing for stand-up animals, pictures, etc.

Catalogs and magazines: save some of these as picture resources for families, clothing, homes, etc. *National Geographic Magazine*, although for adults in content, is a good resource for places, animals, and people.

Cheap white paper: you can buy this by the ream at office supply stores.

Coloring books: animals, holidays, etc. as pattern resources.

Construction paper: large 18" x 24" multi-colored pads are invaluable.

Crayons: a box of 16 or 24 is enough for a four year old. The big fat ones are nice for younger children. An elementary school art teacher once told me that you should take off all the paper on the crayons, so the child can use both the small tip and the long sides to cover—it's true!

Dried beans, peas, macaroni, etc.: used in collages, fish and turkey pictures, etc.

Glitter and sequins: these are optional. They are messy, but fun from time to time especially on December activities.

Glue gun: also good for quick drying jobs. Keep the hot gun away from your child.

Glue stick: easy for younger children to handle when gluing.

Glue: a quick-drying "craft" or "tacky" glue is best. It is available at most craft or hobby stores. It is thicker than ordinary glue and dries more quickly.

Ink pad: used for fingerprint animals, vegetable printing, etc. Make sure you use ones with washable ink. Crayola® makes a nice one.

Markers: you'll use these mainly to draw the outlines of pictures that the child will then color. Washable ones are easier to clean up in case of accidents, but they also smudge more easily when using. You will need to make the choice.

Pipe cleaners: these come in handy for insect feelers, Christmas decorations, animals, etc. I like having a lot of white ones that can be colored with a marker or paint, but an assortment of colored ones is nice too.

Scissors: your child should learn to use a good, blunt pair of scissors by the time he is four.

Spray adhesive: nice for gluing large sheets of paper to cardboard or construction paper. Use it in the garage or outside, only by you!

Stickers: available from gift shops, craft or hobby stores, stationery and school supply stores. Good for making theme booklets, decorations for holidays, etc. With the great interest in stickers among kids today, you can find just about anything in a sticker form.

Tempera: this can be purchased already mixed in unbreakable bottles from school supply stores. You can also mix up your own from powder and store it in small baby food jars. This paint can be used for every large painting job, and it's washable.

Tissue paper: available from art supply or craft stores. Tissue paper comes in large packages, but I prefer the small 5" square ones that come with several colors in a package.

Wiggly eyes: these plastic eyes come in various sizes and are available at craft or hobby shops. They are fun to use sometimes instead of traditional paper or cutout eyes.

Other items that will appear are:

Acrylic paint
Buttons
Chalk
Clothespins (old fashioned), the wooden kind which do not have a spring
Cording
Cotton balls
Dowels
Drinking straws
Egg cartons
Egg shells
Empty margarine tubs
Fabric scraps
Felt
Florist wire
Food coloring
Glycerin
Ivory soap flakes, for the snow in your winter snow paperweights
Milk cartons
Moth flakes (poisonous), remember not the balls or crystals
Orange juice cans with pull-tab lids
Paper fasteners
Paper plates
Pellon® interfacing: stiff backing available at a fabric store
Pompoms
Popsicle® sticks
Ribbon
Small and large boxes
Stapler
String
Tape
Thumbtacks
Tongue depressors
Toothpicks
Tracing paper
Yarn

Nice to have:

tape recorder
globe
flannel board

RESOURCE MATERIALS

Library:

I can't say enough about how wonderful the library is for your nursery planning and, best of all, it's free. A trip at least once every three weeks will allow you to get the books you need. The librarians will also get to know you and are often willing to help you find things. Many libraries have pictures of many subjects you can check out, as well as appropriate cassette tapes and videos.

Community:

So many people are willing to take the time to share their talents with our children. For example, a friend who is a police officer willingly showed his patrol car, even demonstrating the siren and lights. The firefighters did a lot of extra things for our children, because there were only two of them when we took them for a tour. We also traveled to a nearby farm, where the farmer's wife showed our child her chicken coop, the geese and a cow with her new calf. She even showed our son how she made butter out of cream! We chose a quiet time of the day for our bus ride, and the driver showed what levers he pushed to make the doors open and close and how the token machine worked. Many field trips require a call ahead to set up an appointment—a week's notice is usually fine.

Magazines:

Here are several magazines, which consistently have good material for younger children. Many libraries have magazines in their children's section that can be checked out. If you don't have access to a particular magazine to review before you order a subscription, write and ask them for a sample copy. Many church denominations have publications for children. These have good stories for preschoolers, plus many activities and easy recipes for kids. Check with your minister or rabbi.

Humpty Dumpty
Children's Better Health Institute
P.O. Box 7133
Red Oak, IA 51591-0133

Ladybug - children ages 2–6
P.O. Box 592
Mt. Morris, IL 61054-7824

This publisher also produces *Cricket* magazine for older children. These magazines have well written stories to supplement your materials.

Ranger Rick's Nature Magazine - older children
Your Big Backyard - preschoolers
National Wildlife Federation
1400 Sixteenth St. NW
Washington, D.C. 20078-6420

These magazines have beautiful nature photographs, plus stories and activities. The children love looking at them. If you are looking for visual aid resource material, this magazine is invaluable. I cut them up, placing the appropriate pictures in the different chapter folders. You can also call 1-800-432-6564

Sesame Street Magazine
P.O. Box 2895
Boulder, CO 80321

A colorful magazine for preschoolers using learning concepts and familiar friends from Sesame Street.

Turtle Magazine for Preschool Kids
1100 Waterway Blvd.
Box 567
Indianapolis, IN 46206

This magazine emphasizes health, safety, exercise and good nutrition for preschoolers.

Zoobooks
P.O. Box 85384
San Diego, CA 92186-9708

This magazine covers different animals with many excellent photographs.

Mobiles:

I have found that mobiles are a nice way to display many pictures. Mobiles also keep pictures away from younger brothers and sisters. Here are several kinds, ranging from simple to complex. Feel free to use whichever type is the best for you, regardless of the illustration that might appear next to the activity in the book.

An ordinary coat hanger with yarn hanging down. This can be hung from a ceiling light or a curtain rod.

A cross made from cut pieces of clothes hangers, small wooden dowels, or even soda straws. Tie it firmly in the center and hang from a light or attach to the ceiling with a thumb tack.

The most elaborate kind is made from different length hangers or dowels, loosely joined with yarn, string or fishing line. This is the most attractive mobile, but it takes a little time to adjust the ends so they will balance evenly.

Paper Books:

Children love to make these little books. I take several 2" x 4" pieces of paper, fold them in half and staple the middle. On the front, I write the title (such as "My Butterfly Book"). The child can then fill them with appropriate stickers, glue in pictures, or draw his own pictures on the pages.

Tissue Pictures:

Another fun way to make pictures of holiday decorations is with 1" squares of colored tissue paper, available at an art supply or craft store. These are wrapped around the bottom of a pencil, dipped in quick-drying glue, and then pressed down on a pre-drawn outline. The steps are repeated until the picture is filled in. The child may also want to make abstract color designs.

Collages:
These are pictures made up of photographs or other kinds of material. For instance, when talking about fruit, the child can glue many pictures of fruit overlapping each other onto construction paper. You can also use dried beans, scraps of fabric, cotton balls—anything that can be glued down will work in a collage (when gluing heavy items, you made find that a glue gun works better because it lays down a thick layer).

Matching Games:
Make small cardboard game boards with squares for the number of different stickers or pictures you have. Place a different sticker in each square. Mount matching stickers on small cardboard squares. The child then must place each small square over the matching square on the board. From time to time in the book, there will be patterns to draw onto the squares.

POST SCRIPT

Here are just a few final hints to help things run more smoothly for you:

- **Relax:** remember that the purpose of this book is not to push your child into doing things he isn't ready for. Let him learn new concepts when he's ready for them. (By the way, the "he" referred to throughout the book can also be changed to "she" depending on the sex of your child!)

- **Be Flexible:** if you're about to study winter and days are balmy and warm, substitute another chapter (unless, of course, your winters are always balmy and warm!) Come back to the winter chapter when the weather changes.

- **Be Patient:** especially the first month, you'll notice your child's attention span will probably be quite short—a five to ten minute lesson and a ten minute craft may be enough. By the end of the year, the child will usually want things to go on all day!

- **Avoid Distractions:** it is terribly frustrating for both your child and you to have phone interruptions, etc. Take the phone off the hook or turn the bell down, so you can't hear it. Soon, others will know when you cannot be disturbed.

- **Be Willing to Share:** include other children in your activities, from time to time, if you are not already doing so. Field trips are a good time to do this. Parties are much more fun when others are included, and there are several parties scheduled for days when we talk about the holidays.

- **Have Fun:** remember that the whole point about your time with your child is to help him love to learn, to do things, to enjoy books, etc. Don't let the mechanics spoil that!

TREATS	ARTWORK, CRAFT, PROJECTS	FINGERPLAY, RECORD, SONG	BOOKS	INTRO	
					MONDAY
					WEDNESDAY
					FRIDAY

SUBJECT:

CHAPTER 3
ME AND MYSELF

In this chapter the child will learn his name and age and will have the opportunity to explore the many things that he can do with his body, both in play and in everyday experiences.

DAY 1
MY NAME AND AGE

MATERIALS
Tape recorder and tape
Plain paper, glue

Snack: pretzels or cookie
dough

PROJECTS
Growth Chart: commercial or homemade (48" x 5" strip of newsprint, paper
    measuring tape, glue) growth chart
Birthday Cake: pattern for each child cut from white construction paper,
    paper candles, crayons
Name Plates: white construction paper, crayons

In advance, make a tape recording reciting lots of different children's
names. When your child hears his name, he should stand up. Then have
the recording give directions of something to do after hearing his name:
"John, march around," or "Jennifer, jump up and down," etc. Have him
follow the directions.

If he isn't already doing it, now is a good time for him to learn to write
his name. Start by writing the child's name in large letters, both upper
and lower case. Have him trace the letters several times. Then have him
practice writing each letter individually. (It's more fun if the child can
use a different colored crayon for each letter.)

Talk about what "birthday" means, and how we measure his age. Ask
him, "How old are you?" and help him respond.

Show pictures of the child at different ages. Kids always love to talk
about themselves as babies.

Help the child tell a story about himself: "Once upon a time, there was a
little boy/girl named _____, who was _____ years old," etc.
Help him include facts about himself, and the things he like to do.
Sometimes, it helps for you to tell a story about the child first, so he
understands the idea.

A Birthday for Frances, Russell Hoban
Big Beds, Little Beds, Dorothy Z. Seymour
Big, Bigger, Biggest, Edward Dolch
I'm Glad to be Me, P.K. Hallinan
The Birthday Party, Ruth Krauss

Happy Birthday Song

Happy Birthday to you.
Happy Birthday to you.
Happy Birthday dear _____   (Say child's name)
Happy Birthday to you.

This might be a fun time to play marching music. Ask the child to hop,
skip, or jump to the music, according to his name and age—a three-year-
old, a four-year-old, anyone named Melissa, etc. Of course, if you just
have one child doing this, he will think it's funny having you name other
names besides his own.

A Birthday Cake

Today is (child's name) birthday.
Let's make her (or him) a cake.
We'll stir it and mix it   (show stirring)
And then it can bake.   (place cake in oven)
Here's our cake, it looks so nice. (make circle with arms)
The frosting we'll put on   (pretend to frost cake)
And sing a birthday song   (pretend to blow out candles)

Growth Chart

Measure the child on a growth chart on the wall. This can be ready-made or homemade. To make one, cut a strip of newsprint, 48" by 5" and glue a paper measuring tape along one side. This can be decorated as desired. Weigh him, too. Write this information by his height and mark the date. This is a fun activity to repeat a number of times throughout the year.

Birthday Cake Card

Make a birthday cake card for the child out of white construction paper. Put name, age, height, and weight on it. Have the child color the candles (put the correct number for each age), cut each out separately and glue on the cake. Display this in the child's room.

Name Plates

Let the child color in the letters of his name on a piece of white paper. Then he can place the sign by different things in the house that are his. (You can make a number of these, and they can be taped to different belongings for a day or two.)

Help the child make his initials out of pretzel or cookie dough (recipes in Appendix). He can make some for the whole family if you would like.

DAY 2
PARTS OF MY BODY

MATERIALS
Doll
Pictures of body parts (drawn
  or cut from magazine)
Flannel board or large piece
  of cardboard to display pictures
Magnifying glass

PROJECTS
Fingerprint Art: blank sheets of paper, ink pad
Paper Child Puzzle: large sheets of butcher paper, crayons,

Snack: gingerbread men cookies

Begin by describing the child's physical characteristics and letting the child guess who it is. Talk about the color of his eyes and hair, height, clothes, etc. If you have several children, this can be repeated with all of them.

Ask what a "body" is. Help him understand that it's everything from head to toe.

Put pictures of parts of the body on a board or flannel board. Ask him what they are.

Show him a doll. Have him name each part of your body as you point to it. Then have him do so on his own body. This is easier for him the first time if you go from head to toe: head, hair, eyes, nose, ears, mouth, chin, neck, shoulders, etc. Then repeat, calling out different parts at random.

Draw a stick figure, leaving off the head. Ask what is missing. Repeat several times, leaving off different parts.

Have him look at his fingerprints through a magnifying glass. Talk about the fact that everyone has different fingerprints which make him special.

About Me, Jane Moncure
The Foot Book, Dr. Seuss
The Shape of Me and Other Stuff, Dr. Seuss
The Very Little Boy, Phyllis Krasilovsky
Tiny Toes, Donna Jakob

Head, Shoulders, Knees, and Toes (music in Appendix)

(Point to each body part as you sing about it)
Head, shoulders, knees, and toes.
Knees and toes, knees, and toes.
Head, shoulders, knees, and toes,
Eyes, ears, mouth, and nose.

Pointing

Point to your head. Now point to your nose.
Point to your knees. Then point to your toes.
Point to your leg. Now point to your eye.
Point to your elbow and then to your thigh.

Harry and Chester

Hello Harry	(point to hair)
How's Chester	(point to chest)
He just got back from the front.	(point to back, then front)
His feet were needed in the Army.	(point to feet, knees, then arms)
Hip, hip, hooray!!	(hands on hips then raise in air)

Your Hands

Open, shut him; open, shut him;
Give a little clap.
Open, shut him; open, shut him;
Lay him in your lap.
Creep him, creep him way up to your chin!
Open wide your mouth but do not let him in.

Me

Ten little fingers	(Hold up fingers)
Ten little toes	(Point to toes)
Two little ears	(Point to ears)
And one little nose.	(Point to nose)
Two little eyes	(Point to eyes)
One mouth	(Point to mouth)
And a chin	(Point to chin)
It's a big secret, But I'll let you in.	
It's me!!	(Point to whole body)

Fingerprint Art

Use an ink pad, including different colors of ink if desired, and blank sheets of paper. To help the child avoid getting the ink from his fingers all over, you can moisten a cotton ball with nail polish remover, so his fingers can be wiped off immediately after stamping the pad. Let him make shapes or designs. You can draw in features as shown, creating an ant, turtle, owl, mouse, bee, frog, etc.

Child Puzzle

Draw around the child on butcher paper. Have the child color in his face and the clothes he is wearing. Display it for the rest of the chapter. Or cut into a puzzle and let the child put it together.

Make gingerbread men cookies and decorate them.

MATERIALS

Pictures of people cut from
magazines, especially children,
doing things
Snack: taffy, cookies, vegetables

PROJECTS

Body Collage: white paper, pictures of body parts, glue, white paper, pictures
of people doing things, or drawn stick figures
Daily Activity Booklet: 4" x 11" strip of paper, marker, crayons
Mirror: Cardboard, aluminum foil or dime store mirror, glue, pen

Show pictures from magazines or books of a child "doing things." Ask
what the child is doing in each picture. Ask what part or parts of his
body he is using for each activity.

Have the child do movements with his body. Then ask him what part of
his body he is using. For instance: "Jump up and down. Now what are
you using?" (Your legs). Try having the child can swing his arms, wiggle
his fingers, and nod his head.

Play "What do we do with it?" We hear with our _____; we see with
our _____; we chew with our _____; etc. Repeat using incorrect
statements, for example, "We smell with our feet," and let him correct
you.

Ask him to name the things he can do by himself, such as wash his
hands, brush his teeth, pick up toys, etc.

Help him notice the parts of our bodies that help us move—our joints
(elbows, knees, wrists, knuckles, ankles, shoulders).

Hop, Skip and Jump Book, Jack Kent
I Can, Can You?, Ada Litchfield
Is It Hard, Is It Easy, Mary M. Greer
The Run, Jump, Bump Book, Robert Brooks
**The Running, Jumping Throwing, Sliding, Racing, Climbing
Book,** Oscar Weigle

Mirror

Make a "mirror" out of cardboard for the child. The "face" can be made
by gluing in aluminum foil or having the child draw his own face. On the
handle of the mirror you can write his name and age, or the list of things
the child told you earlier that he can do by himself. This little poem can
be put on the other side:

"When I look in the mirror, what do I see?
A smiling face looking back at me.
That face looks so nice,
Now who could it be?
Well, what do you know?
That face must be me!"

Body Collage

Make a collage of body-part pictures cut from magazines. This can include eyes, noses, ears, mouths, arms, hands, legs, etc.

Body Booklet

Have the child make a little booklet with pictures of people (preferably boys and girls) running, throwing, sleeping, etc. He can use the pictures from the introduction or you can draw stick figures that they can color. (See Chapter 2, Teaching Aids, for basic booklet instructions.)

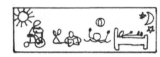

Daily Activity Booklet

Cut a strip of paper, 4" x 11". Make a small chart with the sun on one side and the moon on the other. Draw little stick figures of what the child tells you they do during the day. Have the child color it.

Have the child make taffy (recipe in Appendix) and talk about using his arms and hands to pull and stretch it.

Make cookies and let the child roll out the dough. Talk about how he uses his hands and arms to do this.

Make a vegetable tray. The child can help peel the carrots and cucumbers if you hold his hand as he holds a vegetable peeler. If you make a dip to use, he can shake it or stir it for you.

DAY 4
FACIAL EXPRESSIONS

MATERIALS
Mirror
Pictures cut from magazines
   or drawn of different objects
Tape recorder (optional)

PROJECTS
Happy-Frowny Face: paper plate, marker
Face Game: cardboard, marker, pencil

Snack: sugar cookie faces

Have the child look in a mirror. (Give him a hand mirror or have him stand in front of a bathroom mirror or some other large mirror.) Ask him to look surprised, angry, happy, sad, etc.

Still in front of the mirror, show pictures of different things. Let the child show on his face how each picture makes him feel, such as a birthday cake, a present, a rainy day, or a dog.

Make a list drawing a happy face on one side and a sad face on the other. Ask the child to think of things that make him happy. Then think of things that make him sad.

Use a tape recorder to play back crying, yelling, laughing, giggling, and other vocal sounds. Have the child name the emotion that he hears. Then you name an emotion, and record the child making that sound. Let him hear himself. (If you don't have a tape recorder, you can make the sounds at first, and then let the child make them.)

Alexander and the Terrible, Horrible, No Good, Very Bad Day,
   Judith Viorst
Where the Wild Things Are, Maurice Sendak

If You're Happy and You Know It

If you're happy and you know it, make a grin,
If you're happy and you know it, make a grin,
If you're happy and you know it,
Then your face will surely show it,
If you're happy and you know it make a grin.

(Repeat with other verses:
"If you're sad and you know it, make a frown."
"If you're sleepy and you know it, make a yawn."
"If you're angry and you know it, make a scowl," etc.)

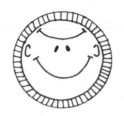

Happy-Frowny Face

Make a happy-frowny face (see illustration) for the child on a paper plate. Cut out eye holes in the middle. Let the child dance around, changing the face and his actions accordingly.

Face Game

Have the child make and color a "Face Game" to play. Cut out a hexagon and have the child color in six faces. Insert a short pencil through the center. Spin it like a top and take turns imitating the facial expression shown when it stops.

Bake already prepared, round sugar cookies (recipe in Appendix) or use refrigerator cookie dough available in the dairy section of your grocery store. Let the child frost them and put different faces on them with cinnamon candies or raisins.

Spread peanut butter on a cracker. Add a face with raisins, peanuts, etc.

MATERIALS

Boxes or bags
Pictures of ear, nose, mouth, hand, eye
Tape recording of different sounds

PROJECTS

Face Plate: paper plate, glue, pictures of facial features
Senses Game: index cards, marker or crayon

Show picture of ears, a nose, a mouth, hands, and eyes. Let the child talk about what each can do.

Mark little bags or boxes with the names of the various senses. Fill each with some of the items listed or add your own. These should be prepared ahead of time for each sense. Blindfold the child (except for the "eyes" bag), and let him guess what is in each bag. If he doesn't want to be blindfolded, he can just close his eyes.

Hearing: Rattle, bell, watch or clock, whistle, aluminum foil to crush or rattle, radio, silverware, seeds or beans in a box to shake.

Smell: Orange, banana, a match after the flame has been blown out, ammonia, perfume, flower, pine (candle or scent).

Taste: Apple, peppermint candy, cracker, peanut butter, jelly, licorice, lemon, pickle, salt, sugar, ice cream or something cold, cocoa or something warm.

Touch: Piece of cloth, round rubber ball, sand, sticky tape, ice, sandpaper, glass surface (mirror or bottle), shell, broom straw, feather, piece of fruit (orange, apple, banana).

Sight: Picture of a rainbow or butterfly, things to view through a piece of colored glass or colored cellophane, a magnifying glass to look at his skin, kaleidoscope.

Tape record sounds and see if he can name what he hears: running water, emptying ice from an ice tray, opening the refrigerator door, the door bell, etc.

Do You Know What I Know?, Helen Borton
Five Senses, Tasha Tudor
Hailstones and Halibut Bones, Mary O'Neill
If You Listen, Charlotte Zolotow
Listen! Listen!, Ylla

My Senses

(Point to each part as you talk about it).
My tongue can taste.
My eyes can see.
My nose can smell wherever I may be.
My fingers touch.
My ears can hear.
My body lets me know about whatever may appear.

Face Plate

Have the child glue pictures cut from magazines of eyes, ears, nose, and mouth onto a round circle face or paper plate putting them where they belong.

Senses Game

Cut plain index cards in half and draw eyes, ears, noses, mouths and hands on different cards. Have the child color them. He can then play a game by drawing a card and naming something that he can see, smell, etc., with that sense.

Let the child eat some of the food that he has previously tasted or smelled.

DAY 6
CLOTHES WE WEAR

MATERIALS
Pictures of different articles of clothing

Clothing in garbage bag or box

PROJECTS
Paper Dolls: construction paper, crayons, glue, fabric

Snack: cookies

Show pictures of different articles of clothing. Have the child name each one. (Catalogs are great sources for these.)

Pull clothing out of a large bag and let the child put each piece on. This is especially fun if you put in Daddy's big boots, a costume clown hat, Mommy's gloves or other articles of clothing he wouldn't ordinarily wear.

Talk about the different kinds of clothes we wear depending on the weather—jackets, snow pants, hats, and gloves in winter; shorts and swimsuits in summer, etc. Talk about what kinds of clothes we wear at different times of the day—pajamas or nightgowns at night, play clothes for outside with friends, special clothes for church or parties.

Talk about each part of the body and what we wear on it: head—hat or ear muffs: hands—gloves or mittens: body—shirt or blouse, sweater or jacket; legs—pants or skirt; feet—socks, shoes, slippers, or boots. The child can make-believe he is putting on the different articles of clothing as you talk about them.

Aaron's Shirt, Deborah Gould
All Dressed Up & Nowhere to Go, Daniel M. Joseph
Blue Hat, Green Hat, Sandra Boynton
Clothes, Debbie Baily
Clothes, Fiona Progoff
Clothes, Matthew Price
Elizabeth Jane Gets Dressed, Anne Tyrell
How Do I Put It On?, Shigeo Watanabe
Let's Get Dressed, Harriet Ziefert
New Shoes, Sam Vaughn
Oh Lewis, Eve Rice
Purple Sock, Pink Sock, Jonathan Allen
What Will I Wear?, Lyn Calder

Paper Dolls

Make paper dolls and have the child color in the clothes or glue clothes cut from fabric onto them.

Make cookies, cutting the dough into shapes of boots, hats, coats, pants, etc.

30

DAY 1	WHO IS IN MY FAMILY?
DAY 2	WHAT FAMILY MEMBERS DO
DAY 3	WHO ARE MY RELATIVES?

In this chapter the child will learn about what a family is and the roles of family members. He will learn about his extended family as well.

DAY 1
WHO IS IN MY FAMILY?

MATERIALS
Pictures of people of different ages
Pictures of family members
Marshmallow People: large
and small marshmallows

PROJECTS
Family Puppets: tongue depressors or Popsicle® sticks, cardboard, pictures
  of family members or drawings by child, toothpicks, crayons, glue
Family Mobile: white poster board, crayons or markers, clothes hanger, thread
  or lightweight string (see general instructions in Chapter 2)

Describe individual family members, such as, "She is in the second grade," " He has brown hair," etc. Ask the child who you are talking about.

Display pictures of people of varying ages (an old catalog or magazine can be an excellent source for these pictures.) Ask the child to identify which look like mothers, which look like fathers, etc. This can be fun if he glues or sticks the pictures onto a larger piece of paper with all the mothers together, all the sisters, etc. Or make different family groups by choosing one picture for a father, one for a mother, and so on.

Show pictures of your family at different ages. When a boy sees his father at his age, it helps him realize that he can be a daddy someday, too.

Be sure to help the child understand that every family is different: some have no daddy or mommy, some have no sisters or brothers, etc. Help the child understand that although each family is different, families are special because of the love they have for one another.

All Kinds of Families, Norma Simon
Are You My Mother?, P.D. Eastman
Big Brother, Charlotte Zolotow
Daddy, Jeanette Caines
Father is Big, Ruth Radlauer
Little Family, Lois Lenski
Mama, Do You Love Me? Barbara M. Joosse
Papa Small, Lois Lenski
Wanted . . . a Brother, Gina Bell
We Have a Baby, Cathryn Falwell
When the Baby Comes I'm Moving Out, Martha Alexander

Finger Family

See my family, see them all	(hold up five fingers)
Some are short,	(thumb up)
And some are tall	(middle finger up)
Let's shake hands—"How do you do?"	(clasp hands, shake)
See them bow—"And how are you?"	(bend fingers)
Father	(middle finger up)
Mother	(pointer finger up)
Sister	(ring finger up)
Brother	(thumb up)
And me	(little finger up)
Together we're a family.	(all fingers up)

Stick Puppets

Make little stick puppets of family members on tongue depressors or Popsicle® sticks. These can be catalog pictures that the child thinks look like the family, or the child can draw them. Mount the pictures on cardboard or have the child draw them directly onto heavy poster board, so they'll stay rigid before gluing to the sticks. The child can make up a little play with the family members talking to one another.

Family Mobile

Make a family mobile using the mobile directions in Chapter 2. Draw a picture of each family member to hang on the mobile. Let the child color the hair and eyes to adapt to each family member. Or if you have photographs, a family photo mobile could be made by gluing the pictures onto cardboard before attaching to the mobile.

Marshmallow People

Provide the child with large and small marshmallows and toothpicks. Let him make marshmallow people of the family. He can save them to show the rest of the family at dinner, or he can eat them now.

DAY 2
WHAT FAMILY MEMBERS DO

MATERIALS
Pictures of family members

PROJECTS
Coupon Book: white paper, pen, markers or crayons
Family Paper Dolls: white construction paper, crayons

Hold up a photo of his father or a picture of a father cut from a magazine and ask the child what he does. Discuss not only what kind of work he does outside the home, but also talk about what he does to help around the house. If there is no father, talk briefly about what fathers in general can do. Repeat for each member of the family.

Have the child pantomime the things that each family member does. Especially talk about the chores each does or responsibilities each has around the house in order to lead up to the activities for this day.

A Father Like That, Charlotte Zolotow
Big Sister, Little Brother, Terry Berge
Big Sister, Little Sister, Charlotte Zolotow
Daddies, Dian Curtis Regan
He's My Brother, Joe Lasker
Just Me and My Dad, Mercer Mayer
Mama, Do You Love Me?, Barbara M. Joosee
Ten, Nine, Eight, Molly Bang
The Way Mothers Are, Miriam Schlein

Coupons for Family

Have the child make a coupon for each family member promising to do something to help them. Perhaps he can polish Daddy's shoes (with your supervision, of course!), clean the table for Mommy, empty the garbage for brother, sort sister's hair ribbons, or play with the baby. If possible, let him think of his own ideas.

Family Paper Dolls

Make family paper dolls, one for each member of your family. Have the child color in clothes and add facial features.

Good Deeds

Have the child do a good deed for each family member (such as making a bed, drawing a picture, straightening shoes in the closet, helping put the laundry away). Have him ask the family at dinner to guess what he did for each of them that day.

Have the child decorate a cookie for each family member to share at dinner. The cookies can be decorated with frosting or colored sprinkles.

Or have the children draw the facial features of each family member on oranges with a marker. Each person's orange can be given to them at dinner.

DAY 3
WHO ARE MY RELATIVES?

MATERIALS
Pictures of grandparents
Photographs of child's
  grandparents

PROJECTS
Letter to Grandparents: stationary and stamps
Photo for Grandparents: cardboard frame, crayons, snapshot

Show pictures of a grandfather and a grandmother. Help the child understand who grandparents are.

Show photographs of his grandparents. This is especially important if the grandparents are no longer living, so that the child can understand who they are. Children need to know they still have grandparents, even if they are no longer alive.

If possible, show photographs of yourself as a child with your parents. Help the child understand who his grandparents are in relation to him.

Talk about things grandparents do. If they live in a different city and the child doesn't visit with them frequently, talk about the things their grandparents do each day—things such as eating breakfast and cleaning the house and also their hobbies, jobs and other interests they have where they live.
Now is a good time, if the child is not as close to one set of grandparents as the other, to help him know more about both sets—make sure you give them all equal time!

Help him understand that his aunts and uncles are your brothers and sisters, just as he or his friends have brothers and sisters.

All Kinds of Families, Norma Simon
Grandfather and I, Helen E. Buckley
Grandma Had a Churn, Louise A. Jackson
Grandmother and I, Helen E. Buckley
Grandmother Lucy books, Joyce Wood
Grandmother Told Me, Jan Wahl
Grandpa Had a Windmill, Louise A. Jackson
Grandparents Around the World, Dorka Raynor
Grandpa's Long Red Underwear, Lynn Schoettle
I Have Four Names for My Grandfather, Kathryn Lasky
Mary Jo's Grandmother, Janice M. Udry

My Grandmother

These are grandmother's glasses   (make round circles with fingers)
This is grandmother's cap   (place hands on top of head)
This is the way she folds her hands,   (fold hands in air)
And puts them in her lap.   (rest in lap)

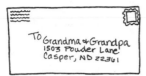

Letter to Grandparents

Have the child draw a picture or dictate a letter to send to his grandparents.

Picture for Grandparents

Have the child decorate a cardboard frame with crayons or a collage of beans. This can be purchased at a photo store or craft store. Place a snapshot of the child inside and give to the grandparents.

A Visit to Grandma's

If grandparents live nearby, a visit can be arranged to their home this day. Or a visit could be made to a nursing home.

Prepare a favorite recipe from a grandparent or other relative.

CHAPTER 5
HOMES

DAY 1	PARTS OF A HOUSE
DAY 2	ROOMS IN A HOUSE
DAY 3	FURNITURE
DAY 4	HOW A HOUSE IS BUILT
DAY 5	OTHER KINDS OF HOUSES
DAY 6	ANIMAL HOMES

In this chapter the child will learn the aspects of a house, including the things that make up a house and how a house is built. He will also learn about other types of houses and homes.

DAY 1
PARTS OF A HOUSE

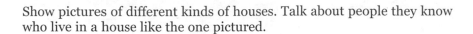

MATERIALS

Pictures of houses (from
magazines or coloring books)
Construction paper
Glue

PROJECTS

House Outline: construction paper, crayons
Toothpick House: construction paper, toothpicks, glue
House Booklet: white paper, yarn or stapler

Show pictures of different kinds of houses. Talk about people they know who live in a house like the one pictured.

On a piece of construction paper make the outline of a house with strips of paper. These can be glued down or just placed on the paper. Make walls, roof, door, chimney, and windows. Help the child learn the names of different parts of the house.

Play a guessing game, saying, for example, "People go through me to get inside a house" (door); "I hold up the roof" (walls).

Describe your house. Let the child guess whose house you are describing. Describe some of his friends' homes. Let him guess whose house you are describing. (You may have to give him lots of hints on this, since children aren't always aware of the physical features of their friends' houses.) You may say, "In this house live three brothers" or "In this house lives a big white dog named Sugar" to get him started.

A House is a House For Me, Mary Ann Hoberman (shows all kinds
of houses)
My House, Miriam Schlein
What is a House?, Richard Scarry
A House For Everyone, Betty Miles

What is this House?

There's a little round house	(form a circle with hands)
With a little yellow (correct color) roof	(place fingers together)
And two windows upstairs to look out.	(make circles with each hand)
There's a latch to loose	(pretend to unlock door)
And a little red door	(pretend to open door)
To walk inside no doubt.	(walk with fingers)
(Child's Name) head is the little house	(point to head)
His (hair color) hair is the roof	(point to hair)
His eyes are the upstairs windows	(point to eyes)
His nose is the latch to loose	(point to nose)
And what do you think is the little door?	
Why (child's name) mouth, of course!	(point to mouth)

House Booklet

Make a little house booklet to be used for the whole chapter. Enlarge the picture onto the lower half of an 8" x 10" piece of paper. Fold in half on the roof line. This is the cover. The child can color this today. (You can either leave the outside margin of the piece of paper as it is or actually cut around it, so that the book looks like a house). On subsequent days, you will add colored paper to match the different rooms in your house. These pages can be stapled together along the roof line, or yarn can be threaded through two holes punched along the top.

(Note: If you have chosen to have the child do this activity, you will want to add it to the supplemental crafts throughout this chapter.)

House Outline

Draw the outline of a house in black on a piece of paper. Let the child color it. Or use toothpicks to make the outline.

With carrot and celery sticks, let the child form a house outline on a plate before eating it. (The vegetables, of course, not the plate!)

MATERIALS

PROJECTS
House Booklet: construction paper, glue

Describe a room in the house. You may want to mention the colors of the room, the furniture in it, and the activities performed in it. Let the child guess which room it is.

Talk about how we use each room. Act out what we do in each room. The child might even want to show how we clean each room: vacuum, scrub the floor, etc.

Tell the child you are going to talk about the things we do in each room, but that you will mix them all up. Say, for example, "We sleep in the kitchen," "We take baths in the living room," and let the child correct you.

This might be a good time to review any rules you have for your house, such as not running inside, only eating in the kitchen, etc. (Whatever the rules are in your house!).

A Place to Stay, Frank Jupo
The Little House, Virginia Burton
A Little House of Your Own, Beatrice DeRegniers and Irene Haas

My House

I have a nice house.
Here is the floor.
Here are the walls.
The roof,
And the door.

(hold palms out flat)
(intertwine fingers together)
(place fingertips together)
(hold hands open, then clap)

Choose a Room

Let the child choose something to make or do for a room in the house, such as pick flowers for a vase, dust the furniture, vacuum, or draw a picture to hang on the wall.

House Booklet

Make the room pages for your house booklet. Try to choose colors of paper that correspond to the colors of specific rooms in your house—if the bedroom is blue, choose blue paper, for instance. Write down the name of the room at the bottom of each page.

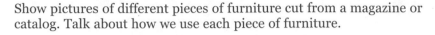

MATERIALS

Pictures of furniture (cut from magazines or catalogs)

PROJECTS

Furniture and Room Pictures: pictures of furniture, construction paper, glue
Furniture Booklet: furniture pictures or drawings of furniture, glue
Cardboard Furniture: lightweight cardboard, markers, empty spools

Show pictures of different pieces of furniture cut from a magazine or catalog. Talk about how we use each piece of furniture.

Describe a piece of furniture. Let the child guess what it is.

Talk about the different parts of a piece of furniture. For instance, with a chair, show the back, the legs and the seat. (Use doll house furniture or the furniture in your home.)

Place doll furniture or pictures mounted on cardboard in a bag. As the child removes them one at a time, let him tell what each is and where it goes.

Have him pantomime being a piece of furniture: a chair, a table, a bed. Kids really love this if you help them get started.

A People House, Theo LeSeig
At Our House, Lois Lenski
Goldilocks and the Three Bears, various authors
No Jumping on the Bed, Tedd Arnold
Roll Over, Mordecai Gerstein
When I'm Sleepy, Jane R. Howard

Furniture Picture

From the pictures that the child has seen, let him choose furniture that he likes and glue them to a piece of paper.

Room Picture

From pictures, let the child choose all the furniture that goes in the same room and glue to a piece of paper.

Booklet Furniture

Glue or color pictures of furniture in the little rooms in your house booklet.

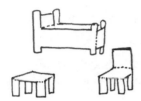

Cardboard Furniture

Out of lightweight cardboard or heavy paper, make little pieces of furniture. These can be painted or colored before assembly. An empty thread spool with a paper cone shade will make a nice lamp.

DAY 4
HOW A HOUSE IS BUILT

MATERIALS

Building materials: brick, rock, wood, nails
Tools: hammer, nails, pliers, sandpaper, saw
Toy trucks

PROJECTS

House Box: shoe box, carpet scraps, wallpaper
Sawdust Picture: sawdust, tempera, glue, colored construction paper
Sandpaper Picture: sandpaper, crayons, paper towels, iron

Talk about some of the things that houses are made of and possibly have materials to show him, such as a brick, a large rock, wood, or shingles.

Discuss tools used in building. Let the child hammer nails into a board, use sandpaper and pliers.

Bring toy trucks like those used in construction. Talk about what they do. (If the weather permits, and you have a sand pile, this could be done outside.)

The Biggest House in the World, Leo Leonni
Around the House that Jack Built, Roz Abisch

Building a House

I'll take a hammer and rap, rap, rap.　　　　(make fist with one hand, pound in palm of other)

With a saw I'll see, saw, see,　　　　(pretend to be sawing)
Now with a brush, I'll paint, paint, paint,　　　　(pretend to be painting.)
To build a house for me.　　　　(clap hands)

Cardboard Box House

Make a little house from a cardboard box. Place carpet scraps inside. Use old wallpaper or wrapping paper for walls. Cut door and windows. Put in the furniture you made in Day 3.

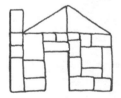

Block House

Have the child build a house with wood blocks or plastic building bricks.

Sawdust Picture

Make sawdust pictures, mixing sawdust (available from a lumber store) with dry tempera to create colors. Let the child make designs with glue; sprinkle sawdust on as desired; blow excess off when dry.

Sandpaper Picture

Make a sandpaper picture. Let the child use crayons to color a picture onto a large piece of sandpaper. Then place a piece of paper towel over the picture and iron at a low setting to set the picture.

Construction Site Field Trip

Visit a construction site to watch the workers at their tasks. Talk about what is going on.

Build a little house out of graham crackers and frosting. Or make a little gingerbread house. (These can be done for any day in this chapter.)

DAY 5
OTHER KINDS OF HOUSES

MATERIALS
Pictures of houses from
   other lands
Pictures of other kinds of houses
   (apartments, mobile homes, etc.)
Snack: Eskimo Igloo Cake

PROJECT
Sugar Cube Igloo: sugar cubes, frosting

Show pictures of homes from other lands: igloos, grass huts, stilt houses, chalets. Encyclopedias and *National Geographic* magazines are good sources for these pictures. Talk about the materials that were used to build these houses, such as ice blocks for the igloo, wood poles for the stilt house, grasses for the Southseas hut, etc. You might also mention why the people living there would have chosen to build the kind of house that they did—climate, materials available, expense, etc.

Ask him what he thinks it would be like living in these kinds of homes. What kinds of clothes would he have to wear? How would the people who own these homes take care of them?

Alfred Goes House Hunting, Bill Binzen
Have You Seen Houses?, Joanne Oppenheim
Houses Around the World, Louise L. Floethe
We Live by the River, Lois Lenski
We Live in the City, Lois Lenski

House Field Trip

Arrange a visit inside an apartment, trailer, or some other kind of home than the one you live in. Talk to the owners about why they like their house.

Drive Field Trip

Take a drive in your car and talk about all the kinds of homes you see.

Sugar Cube Igloo

Let the child help you build an igloo out of sugar cubes and frosting "glue."

Eskimo Igloo Cake

Make a cake shaped like an Eskimo igloo. Cut 2 layer cakes in half, both crosswise and lengthwise; frost three half-layers with white frosting and set all four side-by-side on a plate; frost the outside edges. With melted chocolate or colored frosting, have the child draw the ice blocks onto the white frosting. If you want, you can use a cut-down cupcake for the entrance tunnel. This is fun to make during the day and serve to the whole family that night.

DAY 6
ANIMAL HOMES

MATERIALS
Blanket
Snack

PROJECTS
Animal Homes: play dough
Stick Homes: play dough or clay, sticks

Talk about the different kinds of homes that animals have, such as a beaver dam, a bear cave, a bird nest, and a rabbit burrow. You might also briefly mention beehives and ant colonies, although we will be talking about these in depth in a later chapter.

Talk about why they have that kind of home and how they make it.

Put a blanket or sheet over a table and have the child pretend that he's a little bear in a cave or a bunny in a burrow. Ask him how he would feel in this kind of home. Ask him what he would like about it, and what he wouldn't like.

Does a Mouse Have a House?, Anne Miranda
If You Walk Down This Road, Kate Duke
Pippa Mouse, Betty Boegehold
The Beaver's Pond, Alvin Tresselt
The Brownstone, Paul Scher

Animal Homes

A cave is nice for a big brown bear.	(put arms in a circle)
A bird lives in the tree.	(hook thumbs, flap outstretched fingers)
A hive is the very nicest home For a happy little bee.	(cup hands together)

Hand Houses

Here is a nest for the robin.	(cup hands)
Here is a hive for the bee.	(place fists together)
Here is a hole for the bunny,	(fingers and thumb together to make a circle)
And here is a house for me!	(fingertips together to make a roof)

Play Dough Homes

With play dough (recipe in Appendix) or clay, make different kinds of animals' homes.

Stick Homes

With clay and sticks, let the child build a play beaver's dam or bird's nest.

Eat pretzel sticks pretending that they are the sticks or twigs used for building bird nests or beaver homes.

DAY 1	**WHAT IS FALL?**
DAY 2	**LEAVES**
DAY 3	**WHAT DO PEOPLE AND ANIMALS DO IN FALL?**

In this chapter, the child will learn about the autumn season, how nature changes at this time of the year, and activities that animals and people do in the fall. The child will also have the opportunity to learn or reinforce his knowledge of colors and identify matching shapes.

DAY 1
WHAT IS FALL?

MATERIALS
Construction paper leaves
Leaf shapes
Pine tree branch
Paper bag
Snack

PROJECTS
Pressed leaves: colored leaves, waxed paper, thread
Painted Leaves: leaves, tempera paint
Pine Needle Painting: pine needles, tempera paint

Tell a story about a green leaf changing colors and finally falling off the tree. This can be drawn or told with flannel board pictures. When the tree is preparing for winter, it no longer needs its leaves to provide food for it, so the leaves lose their coloring and drop from the tree. Explain that this falling of leaves is why we call this season "fall."

Show a pine tree branch. Talk about its "leaves"—the needles. Explain why the needles don't fall off. (When you go for your autumn walk, point out various evergreens.)

Talk about the weather in the fall—some days are cool and some days are hot. Explain that the cool weather tells the animals and plants that it is time to get ready for winter. The leaves on the trees start to change color in the fall, the birds fly south, and the squirrels gather food.

Cut leaf shapes out of colored paper and have the child match paper leaves with colored pieces of construction paper. Have him name the colors.

A Pocketful of Seasons, Doris Foster
Fall Is Here, Jane Moncure
Follow the Fall, Maxine Kumin
Now It's Fall, Lois Lenski
The Bears' Almanac, Stan and Jan Berenstein, pp. 54-57

I Like Leaves

I like leaves, all kinds of leaves.
Bright little red leaves,
Quiet little brown leaves,
Happy little green leaves,
Sunny little yellow leaves.
I like leaves, all kinds of leaves.

(Have child hold up the matching leaf as you talk about each color.)

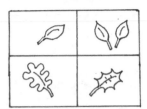

Pressed Leaves

Iron colored leaves between sheets of waxed paper (place a paper towel over and under the waxed paper when ironing.) Cut around them leaving a small margin. These are pretty hanging in a window from different pieces of thread or attached to the glass with cellophane tape.

Painted Leaves

Paint leaves with tempera paints (you may have to press the leaves first with an iron on a low setting). Glue onto a piece of paper.

Pine Needle Painting

Paint with pine needles or use a whole branch as a brush and tempera paints on plain paper.

Fall Walk

Go for a walk. Have the child collect a bag of different colored leaves for Day 2's activities. You can also make this into a scavenger hunt by asking him to collect certain things that are symbols of fall, such as acorns, colored leaves, seeds, pine cones, nuts, and cocoons (you will want to have him just show you these, or you can carefully put them in a jar with air holes in the lid, leave them in a cool place and watch what hatches in the spring when the weather warms up).

DAY 2
LEAVES

MATERIALS
Tree picture
Autumn leaves (from Day 1)
Snack

PROJECTS
Leaf Rubbings: leaves, white paper, crayons
Leaf Collage: construction paper, leaves
Leaf Mobile: colored construction paper leaves, pipe cleaners, glue
    (see general directions in Chapter 2)

Draw a large picture of a tree on newsprint and tape it to the wall. Have the child glue or tape paper or real leaves to it.

Have the child look at the leaves you gathered. Have him make a pile of each color. Let the child count the leaves and match the shapes.

Have the child look at the veins in the leaves. (This works best with leaves that are not very dried out). Explain that the food for the tree is made in the leaves by mixing sunshine and water. Then the food travels to the rest of the tree through the veins. Show him that the veins in a leaf are like his own veins (the ones at his wrist are the easiest to identify.)

All Falling Down, Gene Zion
Johnny Maple Leaf, Alvin Tresselt

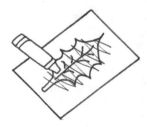

Bright Leaves (fingerplay and song - see Appendix)

See the bright leaves on the trees   (Pretend to be trees)
Rustling in the autumn breeze   (Wave arms back and forth)
Whirling, twirling through the air   (Turn around like leaves)
Fall here and there.   (Fall on the floor)

Have the child pretend he is a leaf and have him dance to music.

Leaf Rubbings

Make leaf rubbings from your collected leaves. Put a leaf under a piece of paper. Rub over the paper with the side of a crayon, until an imprint comes through. Several rubbings can be done on one piece of paper using different shaped leaves and different colored crayons.

Leaf Collage

Make a collage of leaves on a piece of construction paper.

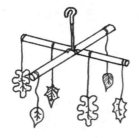

Leaf Mobile

Make a leaf mobile (see general directions in Chapter 2). Cut different shaped leaves out of colored construction paper, or use white paper and have the child color the leaves. The leaves are extra pretty if you glue matching colored pipe cleaners around the outside of each leaf.

Talk about and then eat edible "leaves" such as lettuce, spinach, and cabbage.

DAY 3
WHAT DO PEOPLE AND ANIMALS DO IN THE FALL?

MATERIALS
Pictures of animals that hibernate
Snack

PROJECTS
Tissue Trees: white paper, brown crayons, tissue paper in autumn colors
Weather Chart: white paper, crayons

Show pictures of animals that live in winter, such as bears, rabbits, squirrels, and insects.

Talk about how animals store food and dig homes in the ground, their fur gets heavier, bears eat a lot, etc.

Talk about what people do to get ready for winter: harvest their crops, protect their plants, rake the leaves, clean their gardens—whatever you do.

How Animals Hide, Robert M. McClung (a National Geographic
                 Society Young Explorer book)
Sleepy Time, Eva Evans
The Tale of Squirrel Nutkin, Beatrix Potter
The Tale of the Grasshopper and the Ant, various authors
Wake Up, Groundhog!, Carol Cohen
Where Does Everyone Go?, Aileen Fisher

Autumn is a Special Time

When autumn comes, it's a special time
Our yard we clean and rake   (pantomime cleaning and raking)
We gather all the leaves around   (make a big circle with arms)
And a great big pile we make—jump! (on the word "jump," pretend to
                                       jump into a pile of leaves)

Leaf Jumping

Rake leaves in a big pile outside and let the child run and jump into them.

Tissue Trees

Have the child color outlines of tree trunks brown, and then glue little torn tissue colored "leaves" on them (see general tissue picture directions in Chapter 2)

Weather Chart

Make a weather chart where he can keep track of the weather for this week or for several weeks. This will help him be aware of the changing fall weather.

Eat apples or applesauce.

DAY 1	FRUITS
DAY 2	VEGETABLES
DAY 3	MILK AND DAIRY PRODUCTS
DAY 4	MEAT AND FISH
DAY 5	GRAINS
DAY 6	WATER

In this chapter the child will learn about the different food groups and where they come from.

DAY 1
FRUITS

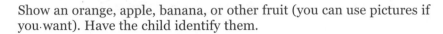

MATERIALS
Different kinds of fruit: both
   real and pictures of fruit
Snack

PROJECTS
Fruit Matching Game: white paper, crayons
Fruit Puzzles: white construction paper, crayons

Show an orange, apple, banana, or other fruit (you can use pictures if you·want). Have the child identify them.

Put the fruit into a bag and let the child guess what each one is by feeling it and not seeing it.

Talk about how each fruit is different. An apple has a smooth skin that can be eaten. If you cut an apple in half cross-wise, the child can see the little star made by the seeds in the center. An orange skin has little bumps on it and has to be peeled before you can eat the fruit. A banana has to be peeled, too, and the seeds are so little they can be eaten. (You might want to put a banana in the refrigerator for a few days until the skin turns black, but—surprise!—the inside is still perfect for eating). Discuss other fruit as you wish.

Talk about the fact that not all fruit grows on trees. Berries and pineapple grow on bushes, and melons and grapes grow on vines.

A Friend for Dragon, Dav Pilkey
An Apple a Day, Judith Barrett
Blueberries for Sal, Robert McCloskey
Food, Irving Adler
Fresh Cider and Pie, Franz Brandenberg
Good Lemonade, Frank Asch
The Beetle Bush, Beverly Keller (a great story about a watermelon)
The Blueberry Pie Elf, Catherine Wooley
Who's Got the Apple?, Jan Loot

Fruit Matching Game

Using magazine pictures or stickers, have the child match all the pictures of fruit that are red, then yellow, then purple, then green, then orange. If you want, the pictures can be glued on separate pages and made into a book.

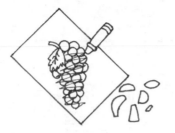

Fruit Puzzles

Draw pieces of fruit onto white construction paper cut in half. Have the child color each one the correct color for the fruit. Cut the pictures into several pieces depending on the age and ability of the child. Mix up the pieces and have the child first match the colors and then put each piece of fruit back together.

Farmer's Market

Visit a farmer's market and see all the fruit (and other food) on display.

Cider Mill or Apple Orchard

Visit an orchard or a cider mill.

Make a fruit salad using as many fresh fruits as possible.

Have apple or orange juice.

DAY 2
VEGETABLES

MATERIALS
Many varieties of vegetables or
  pictures of vegetables
Snack

PROJECTS
Celery Painting: celery stalks with leaves, tempera paint, construction paper
Vegetable Printing: white paper, sponge, tempera paint or ink pad
Vegetable Man or Woman: construction paper, glue

Repeat Day 1, using vegetables. Have the child identify different vegetables either by taste or touch.

Talk about the way vegetables grow. Some are called "root" vegetables, because they grow underground. Examples of root vegetables are carrots, radishes, potatoes, turnips and beets. Other vegtables, such as beans, peas, and cucumbers, grow on bushes or vines. Others are nearly the whole plant, such as cabbage, cauliflower, spinach and lettuce. Some are called "leafy vegetables," such as lettuce and spinach.

Have the child break beans into pieces for cooking, open pea pods to remove the peas, or husk corn.

Match vegetables by color, just as you did with fruit.

Autumn Harvest, Alvin Tresselt
Bear and Bunny Grow Tomatoes, Bruce Koscieniak
Blue Bug's Vegetable Garden, Virginia Poulet
The Carrot Seed, Ruth Kraus
Food, Irving Adler
Lentil Soup, Joe Laski
The Great Big Enormous Turnip, Aleksei Tolstoy

Celery Painting

Paint a picture with a celery stalk and tempera using the leaves as bristles. The painting won't look great, but it's lots of fun.

Vegetable Man or Woman

Make a vegetable man or woman out of colored construction paper. Using appropriate colors, cut out a tomato for a head, potato for a body, pea pods for arms, carrots for legs and radishes for feet. Peas can be used for eyes and the nose and mouth can be drawn on.

Vegetable Printing

Cut the leafy ends or stems off various hard vegetables, such as carrots, celery, radishes, or potatoes. Press vegetable against a sponge saturated with paint or an ink pad. Stamp a design onto paper. You can also carefully cut a design into the end of the vegetable, which can be stamped onto paper.

Visit a Pumpkin Patch

Since this is the time of year when pumpkins are ripe and ready to pick, visit a farm or garden where lots of pumpkins are growing. This might also be a time to get your Halloween pumpkin rather than waiting until the week of Halloween.

Using the vegetable person outline above, have the child make a vegetable man or woman out of real vegetables and eat him.

Cut vegetables into different shapes for the child to eat: carrot "pennies," celery "moons," broccoli "trees," radish "flowers," etc.

Make vegetable soup (recipe in Appendix). Have the child help you as much as he is able. He especially would enjoy adding the cut up vegetables to the soup liquid.

MATERIALS

Picture of a cow
Pictures or examples of various
  dairy products

PROJECTS

Homemade Butter: heavy cream, mixer
Homemade Ice Cream: ingredients, freezer

Show a picture of a cow—explain that milk comes from a cow. The child can pretend he is milking a cow. Tell him what happens to the milk after it leaves the cow. The milk is pasteurized and placed in sterilized containers, then it is sent to the store or the milk man delivers it to your door.

Show pictures of different dairy products and explain how they are made. Cheese is made by letting the milk sour until it comes together in solid pieces called curds. The liquid is drained off and the curds are pressed together to form the cheese. Cream is the thick, fattier part of the milk that rises to the top when the milk is left standing for awhile. Butter is made by making or shaking cream until the fat comes together and forms butter.

Ice cream is made by putting cream, sugar, and eggs in a freezer. Nuts or fruit can be added, too. The freezer is placed inside a bucket filled with ice and salt. Then a crank turns a paddle inside the freezer, so that the mixture freezes evenly. (NOTE: this information may be a little beyond the understanding of most preschoolers, so don't feel you have to explain unless the child asks.)

Milk, Butter & Cheese: the Story of Dairy Products, Carolyn
     Meyer
Food, Irving Adler
Some Cheese for Charles, Helen Buckley
The Land Where the Ice Cream Grows, Anthony Burgess
The Old Man Who Loved Cheese, Garrison Keillor

Dairy Visit

Visit a dairy and watch the cows being milked and the milk containers being filled.

Homemade Butter

Whip heavy cream using an electric mixer or food processor until it turns into butter (children love doing this!)

Ice Cream

Make homemade ice cream (recipe in Appendix).

Any dairy product is appropriate for this day. If you have whipped cream into butter, this would be especially fun for him to try on bread.

Cream cheese with jelly on toast is another suggestion.

DAY 4
MEAT AND FISH

MATERIALS

Pictures of cattle, sheep, pigs, poultry, and fish

Pictures of different cuts of meat (cookbooks often have them)

PROJECTS

Hot dog racers: hot dog, bun, carrot, toothpick, olive

Show pictures of different animals and discuss the meat we get from them: cattle—hamburger, hotdogs, steak; sheep—lamb chops, mutton; pig—pork, bacon, ham; poultry—chicken, turkey; etc.

Also, explain that we get eggs from chickens, too. Talk about all the different ways we cook eggs.

Fish and shellfish can also be mentioned as meat sources.

Hold up a picture of each animal and have the child tell you what we get from each animal.

Show pictures of different cuts of meat and talk about how we eat them. The child can pretend he is grilling the hamburger, basting the turkey, scrambling the eggs, etc.

Cloudy with a Chance of Meatballs, Judi Barrett
EAT, Diane Peterson
Food, Irving Adler
Green Eggs and Ham, Dr. Seuss
Mother Rabbit's Son Tom, Dick Gackenbach (about a rabbit who wants to eat hamburgers instead of carrots)
The Egg Book, Jack Kent

Butcher Shop

Visit a butcher shop and have the butcher show the child how he cuts the big pieces of meat into different sizes.

Grocery Store Meat Department

Visit the meat department of your grocery store and talk about all the different kinds of meat.

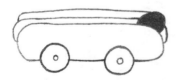

Make hot dog racers for lunch: place heated hot dog in a bun; add four carrot "wheels" attached with toothpicks and an olive "driver."

DAY 5
GRAINS

MATERIALS
Wheat: pictures or kernels
Other grains: oatmeal, rice,
    cornmeal, rye
Snack

PROJECTS
Grain Collage: cardboard, glue, grains (see Materials, p. 11)

Show pictures of wheat or actual kernels of wheat. Have the child pretend he is grinding the wheat to make flour and then making bread.

Talk about other kinds of grains and how we eat them: oatmeal—cereal, cookies; rice—cooked, puddings; corn—tortillas, cornbread; rye—bread. Popcorn can also be mentioned.

Bread and Jam for Frances, Russell Hoban
Clabber Biscuits, Ida Chittum
Food, Irving Adler
Little Bear's Pancake Party, Janice
Noodles, Sarah Weeks & David A. Carter
Pancakes, Pancakes, Eric Carle
Sam's Sandwich, David Pelham
The Giant Jam Sandwich, John Lord and Janet Burroway
The Little Red Hen, various authors
The Sandwich, Dorothy Seymour

Grain Collage

Make a collage of dried beans, wheat, rice, popcorn, and other grains. This can be done by drawing a picture on a piece of cardboard on which the child can glue the pieces of grain or letting him make up his own designs.

Grinding Wheat

Grind wheat into flour. A food processor or blender will do this if you don't have a grinder. Make bread or muffins with the wheat you have ground.

Make bread. This is especially fun if you have small loaf pans.

Break off little pieces of thawed frozen bread dough or homemade bread dough. Roll flat and fry in oil until light brown. Serve with butter and jam.

Fry wheat kernels in oil until just brown. Serve salted.

Cook popcorn.

DAY 6
WATER

MATERIALS
Flavorings, such as Kool-Aid®,
   honey, extracts
Ice cubes
Sponge
Snack

PROJECTS
Colored Bath and Food Coloring Fun: food coloring
Sidewalk Painting: wide paint brush, bucket

Pour water into a glass; have the child taste it, touch it, smell it, color it, and flavor it with extracts, honey, or Kool-Aid®.

Show ice cubes and explain that they are frozen water. Put one in a saucepan and watch it turn back to water.

Fill a bowl half full of water. Using a sponge, have the child squeeze it out, and then soak the water up again.

Water for Dinosaurs and You, Roma Gans

Food Coloring Fun

Put food coloring into several cups of water, mix them with one another to create new colors.
     1 drop blue plus 2 drops yellow make green
     2 drops yellow plus 1 drop red make orange
     1 drop red plus 2 drops blue make violet
     1 drop green plus 4 drops yellow plus 3 drops make brown.

Sidewalk Painting

Paint on the sidewalk, using a wide brush and plain water. This can also be done with the food coloring mixtures made in the activity above. The designs will stay until the water evaporates away. (This is fun in the summer, too.)

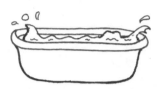

Food Coloring Bath

Have the child take a "colored" bath: put 6-8 drops of food coloring into the bath water. This will not color the child, but makes the bath more fun.

Visit a Lake

Visit a nearby stream, lake or pond. Talk about where the water has come from. If you can visit someone who has a well, it is fun for the child to see how to get water from it.

Have the child help you stir powdered drink mix with water. Pour into ice cube trays and freeze with toothpick handles.

Pour punch or fruit juice over crushed ice in a glass for a "snow cone."

DAY 1	WHAT IS HALLOWEEN?
DAY 2	PUMPKINS
DAY 3	LET'S HAVE A HALLOWEEN PARTY

In this chapter, the child will learn about the holiday Halloween. We put a lot of emphasis on the fun, creative part of this holiday and de-emphasize the macabre side.

DAY 1
WHAT IS HALLOWEEN?

MATERIALS
Commercial Halloween
  decorations
White balloon or cloth,
  black marker
Broom
Snack

PROJECTS
Halloween Matching Games: Halloween stickers, cardboard
Ghost or Pumpkin Balloons: white or orange balloons, black markers

Talk about how Halloween came about. Many, many years ago in England, October 31 was considered the last day of the year, and the people celebrated it sort of like we celebrate New Year's Eve. Witches, ghosts, and other eerie creatures were supposed to come out that day. The next day was a religious holiday, so the "spooks" only had until midnight to play.

Halloween, with all the scary masks and costumes, can be a very frightening experience—especially for young children. It is important to explain that this is all make-believe and not real.

Show a set of commercial Halloween decorations (Hallmark and other card companies make nice ones). Talk about the characters in the pictures.

Draw a ghost face on a white balloon or piece of white cloth draped over your hand and have the ghost "talk" to the child. If the ghost talks funny, tells silly jokes and is friendly, this will allay the child's fears.

Dramatize riding a broom like witches. This is also fun done to music on Day 2.

A Job for Wittilda, Caralyn and Mark Buehner
Clifford's Halloween, Norman Bridwell
Emma, James Stevenson
George and Georgie's Halloween, Robert Bright
Happy Birthday Little Witch, Deborah Hautzig
Little Witch's Big Night, Deborah Hautzig
Suppose You Met a Witch, Ian Serraibbier
The Old Witch Goes to the Ball, Idea DeLage
The Witches Secret, Frances Charlotte Allen
Witch in the House, Ruth Chew

"Danse Macabre" by Saint-Saens is fun music to dance to. The child can pretend he is a witch, a skeleton, or a ghost. He may also want to put a sheet over his head to pretend that he is a ghost. If these are good sheets, you will not want to cut eye holes, but if they are old ones, eye holes make it easier to see.

Halloween Matching Game

Make a matching game with Halloween stickers (see general directions in Chapter 2).

Ghost Balloons

Use black felt markers to make ghost faces on white balloons or jack-o'-lantern faces on orange balloons.

Bake and frost pumpkin cookies or cupcakes using raisins or small candies to make features. You can save some for the party on Day 3.

DAY 2
PUMPKINS

MATERIALS

Orange paper circles, black marker

Brown lunch bag, old newspaper, marker

Orange felt pumpkin, black felt features

Snack

PROJECTS

Jack-O'-Lantern Puppets: tongue depressors, orange paper circles, glue

Talk about the difference between a pumpkin and a jack-o'-lantern.

Cut out orange paper circles; leave some plain and draw jack-o'-lantern faces on others. Hold them up one at a time and have the child tell which are pumpkins and which are jack-o'-lanterns.

Make a jack-o'-lantern puppet by stuffing a brown paper lunch bag with crumpled newspaper and drawing on features. When the features are all drawn on, you can have the puppet "talk" to the child.

Cut a pumpkin shape out of orange felt and place it on a flannel board or the table. Have the child put on different faces using features you have cut out of black felt.

Corduroy's Halloween, Lisa McCue
Halloween with Morris and Boris, Bernard Wiseman
How Spider Saved Halloween, Robert Krauss
It's Halloween, Jack Prelutsky
It's the Great Pumpkin, Charlie Brown, Charles M. Schulz
The Biggest Pumpkin Ever, Steven Kroel

Peter, Peter, Pumpkin Eater

Peter, Peter, Pumpkin Eater
Had a wife and couldn't keep her,
Put her in a pumpkin shell
And there he kept her very well.

Five Little Pumpkins (fingerplay or song - see Appendix)

Five little pumpkins sitting on a gate.
The first one said, "Oh my, it's getting late!"
The second one said, "There are witches in the air!"
The third one said, "I don't care!"
The fourth on said, "Let's run and run and run!"
The fifth on said, "I'm having lots of fun!"
"Woooo," went the wind. Out went the light.
And the five little pumpkins rolled out of sight.

Jack-o'-Lantern Puppets

Cut pumpkin shapes out of orange construction paper and have the child draw faces on them. Attach the pumpkin "heads" to the ends of tongue depressors or craft (Popsicle®) sticks with glue or tape. You can use these puppets to sing the "Five Little Pumpkins" song above.

Pumpkin Buying

Go to a pumpkin farm or grocery store and buy a pumpkin. Bring it back home and carve it. If you don't have a lot of time, buy the pumpkin ahead and just carve it on this day.

Make a pumpkin pie or pumpkin bread.

Fry pumpkin seeds in a little oil until light brown. Salt if desired. (Some of these can also be saved for the party).

DAY 3
LET'S HAVE A HALLOWEEN PARTY

MATERIALS
Brown paper grocery bags
Crayons
Black Cat or Orange Pumpkin
Black and orange construction
   paper
Party Refreshments

PROJECTS
Sucker Ghosts: suckers, facial tissues, thread, marker
Ghoul Pictures: construction paper, tempera paint
Springy Witches: black, green, white construction paper, marker or crayon,
   glue, black yarn

This is a fun day to invite your child's friends to join you.

Decorate brown paper grocery bags for trick or treat bags, using crayons, marking pens, or construction paper cutouts.

Have the children decorate the room with black and orange paper chains. These are made by cutting strips of construction paper lengthwise. Glue the first strip into a circle. Insert the next color through this circle and glue the ends together to make a circle. Continue until the chain is the length you desire.

Make sucker ghosts by covering a round sucker with a white facial tissue. Tie with a thread and draw on eyes with a black marker.

Play "Pin the Tail on the Black Cat" or "Pin the Nose on the Pumpkin," by drawing a large tail-less cat or orange pumpkin on construction paper and hanging on the wall. The tails or noses can be secured with tape which is much safer than the traditional pins.

Have the children decorate pumpkin nut cups as shown for the party table.

The Halloween Party, Lonzo Anderson
The Old Witches Party, Ida Delage
Witch, Goblin, and Sometimes Ghost, Sue Alexander

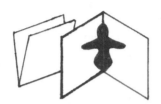

Ghoul Pictures

Make Halloween ghoul pictures by folding construction paper in half, dropping blobs of tempera paint down the center fold and pressing flat. Open up and let dry. Add eyes and a mouth to the finished ghoul.

Springy Witches

Cut a black body and hat and a white or green head out of construction paper, as shown. Draw on a face with black marker or crayon. Fold white paper strips in an accordion-like manner and glue to body for arms and legs. Add paper hands and feet. Hair can be made from pieces of black yarn.

Costume Ideas

In our family, we always have a lot of fun making our own costumes. Sack costumes are easy to make and are very versatile. Fold two yards of material in half and sew side seams, leaving arm holes. Cut two leg holes on the fold side and sew a large seam or cut slits along the top edge to run ribbon cording.

A red bag can be an apple or a tomato; an orange one—a pumpkin; a green one—a monster from outer space; a white one—a rabbit, a snowman, or a mouse; a brown one—a dog or a monkey, or make a giant M&M by adding a "M" to the front of a colored bag. All you have to do is stuff the bag with paper. Add a mask or makeup (see recipe below) and ears or a mop-head wig dyed a matching color.

To make an easy skeleton costume, cut a black garbage bag to fit the child, adding arm and neck holes. Add the "bones" with white contact paper or white plastic tape, and make the skull mask from a paper plate.

Halloween Makeup

> 1 T. white shortening
> 2 T. cornstarch
> 1 tsp. white flour
> 4-5 drops food coloring

Mix together, adding more shortening if needed.

1 T. shortening mixed with 2½ tsp. cocoa makes a great brown all by itself, too.

This makeup can be used for the faces of the bag costumes above. The makeup washes off with soap and water.

Here are some ideas for refreshments at the party:

Make a ghost cake using a cake baked in a 9" x 13" pan. Cut as shown. Use M&M's for eyes inside empty eggshell halves (the egg shells make the ghost look scarier). Licorice string makes the mouth.

Orange Jell-O® (cut in pumpkin shapes with raisin or grape faces added when Jell-O® is partially set).

Orange juice or orange punch.

Licorice.

Nuts or fried pumpkin seeds in nut cups.

Pumpkin cookies, cupcakes, pie or bread saved from one of the previous days.

In this chapter the child will learn about birds, their habits and their characteristics. He should also be able to name several kinds of birds. Library books are good sources for this chapter. Also, *Ranger Rick Magazine* published by the National Wildlife Federation has marvelous color pictures (this is a great magazine to subscribe to for your child anyway). It is available in the juvenile section of most libraries.

DAY 1
WHAT IS A BIRD?

MATERIALS

Pictures of different kinds
   of birds
Sunflower seeds
Bread dough or cookie dough

PROJECTS

Pinecone Feeders: pinecones, peanut butter or melted suet (available at a
   butcher shop or grocery store meat dept.), bird seed, yarn or twine
Rice Cake Rounds: rice cakes, peanut butter, yarn or string
Feather Painting: bird feather, tempera paint, paper
Bird Drawings: pictures from a coloring book or draw outlines of birds
   to color, crayons

Show pictures of different kinds of birds. An encyclopedia or bird book
from the library works well for this. Talk about the birds.

Feathers: If possible, show one and tickle the child gently with it. Talk
about how feathers help the bird fly, how the feathers are sometimes
fluffed out in winter to keep the bird warm and how a water bird's
feathers are waterproof because of the oil in them.

Bill: Talk about how the kind of bill a bird has helps it eat its food. For
example, a woodpecker has to have a sharp bill to peck at trees and get
out insects, a pelican has a large bill which acts like a giant scoop to pick
fish out of the water, a hummingbird has a needle-like bill to suck the
nectar out of flowers, etc.

Feet: Talk about how some birds, such as eagles and hawks, have claws
to help them catch their prey, and others, such as ducks and other water
birds, have webbed feet to help them move through the water.

Tail: Talk about how some birds have long tail feathers which help them
perch, some have fancy tail feathers, such as peacocks, and some have
short little tail feathers such as penguins. Let him pick out the different
kinds of tail feathers from the pictures you show him.

Food: Talk about the different kinds of food that birds eat. For example,
some birds like insects and worms, some like seeds, some like the nectar
of flowers, and some eat small animals such as mice.

Life: Talk about what birds do in the winter, such as fly south, change
their colors to duller shades (such as goldfinches), or change their eating
habits.

Birds, Jane Werner Watson (a Little Golden book)
Flap Your Wings, P.D. Eastman
Recipes for the Birds, Irene and Ed Cosgrove
The Bears' Nature Guide, Stan and Jan Berenstain, pg. 30-33
The Early Bird, Richard Scarry

Black Birds

Two little black birds sitting on a hill,
One named Jack and the other named Jill.
Fly away, Jack. Fly away, Jill.
Come back, Jack. Come back, Jill.

(This is fun to act out by taping two little paper birds on each index finger. Let them "fly away" behind your back and then come back in front of you).

Pine Cones for the Birds

Roll pine cones in peanut butter or melted suet, then roll the pine cones in bird seed. Hang the pine cones on a branch with yarn or twine. The birds may not discover the pine cones right away, so encourage the child to be patient.

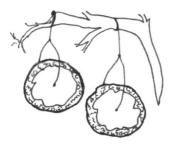

Rice Cake Food

Spread puffed rice cakes with peanut butter. Make a hole in the middle and thread with yarn or string. Hang these outside for the birds–you'll probably find your child loves these, too!

Feather Painting

Paint with a feather, dipping it into tempera paint and brushing across a piece of paper.

Bird Drawings

Have the child color drawings of different birds. These can either be from coloring books or pictures traced out of bird books. Save the pictures to use on Day 4.

Eat toasted sunflower seeds. The child can pretend he is a bird while he does this.

Make birds out of dough—either bread dough or cookie dough works well. Roll dough out to about ½", and cut into strips, 1" x 10". Tie into a knot. Place on cookie sheet in shape shown, squeezing the top to look like a beak. Add a raisin eye. Score the side with a toothpick or skewer to look like feathers. Bake at 375 degrees about 6–8 minutes until golden brown.

DAY 2
NESTS

MATERIALS

Pictures of bird nests or nesting
materials (see Projects)
Old bird nest (optional)
Blankets
Marshmallow Nests: margarine,
miniature marshmallows,
rice cereal
Macaroon Nests: see ingredient list
with activity

PROJECTS

Nest Plaque: walnut shell, small piece of wood, pinto navy beans, florist or
Spanish moss
Nesting Station: grass, twigs, string, yarn, cloth, etc.

Show pictures of bird nests. Talk about the different shapes and how the
nests are attached to the tree branches. Explain that each kind of bird
makes its own kind of nest.

Show grass, twigs, string, and other nest materials. Talk about how birds
weave these together to make their nests.

If possible, show an old nest saved from last summer. If you live in an
area with a lot of birds, old nests are quite easy to find in the late fall
when the leaves have fallen from the trees. In addition, many craft stores
have artificial nests you could use here as well.

Make a "nest" out of blankets. Have the child pretend that he is a baby
bird in the nest. Have him fly away when he thinks he is big enough.

The Best Nest, P.D. Eastman
The Nest Book, Kathleen Daly

Kookaburra (song)

Kookaburra sits in the old gum tree
Eating all the gum drops he can see.
Laugh, kookaburra, laugh, kookaburra,
Save some of them for me.

Miniature Nest Plaque

Make a small nest plaque. Glue half a large empty walnut shell to a piece
of wood; glue several pinto or navy beans inside to look like eggs; florist
moss can be glued around it to look like greenery.

Nesting Materials

On an aluminum pie plate, put different materials that birds like to have in their nest, such as string, thin strips of cloth, small twigs, etc. Put outside in a protected spot, especially by where you put out food for the birds in Day 1's Activities. In just a few days, the items will be taken by the birds.

Marshmallow Treat Nest

¼ c. margarine
3 c. miniature marshmallows
5 c. Rice Crispies, corn flakes, or chow mein noodles

Melt margarine and marshmallows over low heat. Remove from heat and stir in rice cereal. Let it cool a little and shape into small bird nests. You may have to butter the child's hands so that he can form the nests more easily.

Macaroon Nests

1 can sweetened condensed milk
1 14-oz. pkg. shredded coconut
1 tsp. vanilla

Mix all ingredients well. Drop by spoonful onto well-greased cookie sheet. Make an indentation in middle of each cookie to form a "nest." Bake at 325 degrees for 15 min. Cool on cookie sheet 2 min. before removing. (These are very soft cookies so you may have to make another indentation in the cookie when they are cooked.)

(Note: Save some of either of these nests for Day 3.)

DAY 3
EGGS

MATERIALS
Pictures of different kinds of
  bird eggs
Snack: Hard-boiled or
  deviled eggs

PROJECTS
Hatching Bird: white and yellow construction paper, paper fastener, glue
Suet Cakes: peanut butter or melted suet, bird seed, empty egg cartons
Egg Shell Picture: dozen empty egg shells, food coloring, small jar,
  construction paper

Tell the story of how a bird hatches from an egg. Help the child understand that the egg is formed inside the mother with the future baby bird inside. But instead of the bird continuing to grow inside its mother like a human baby, the bird will grow inside the egg. Help him understand that the baby must be kept warm, so the mother (and father) bird sits on the eggs until the babies are ready to hatch. Then the baby birds peck their way out of the eggs. Help him understand that the pecking is also good exercise for the new bird, so the mother will not help with her own beak.

The child may want to pretend he is a baby bird in an egg. Have him scrunch up into a ball and then pretend to peck his way out. You may have to show him how. (Don't be too inhibited; children love it when their parents act and play with them).

If possible, let him see pictures of eggs of different kinds of birds: robin—blue egg; cardinal—lavender speckled egg; mourning dove—white egg; goldfinch—pale blue egg; sparrow—brown egg.

Egg in the Hole Book, Richard Scarry
Egg to Chick, Millicent Selsam
How to Go About Laying an Egg, Bernard Waber
Little Chick's Story, Mary DeBall Kwitz
Make Way For Ducklings, Robert McCloskey
Meg's Eggs, Helen Nicoll
The Pinkish, Purplish, Bluish Egg, Bill Peet

Hatching Bird

Draw an egg on a large piece of white construction paper. Let the child color it any way he likes and cut it out. Then cut a jagged line across the middle and attach the two halves on one side with a paper fastener. Cut a little bird out of either white or colored construction paper, and let the child color. This bird is glued behind the egg, so the bird appears when the egg is "cracked" open.

Egg Shell Picture

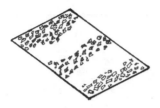

Break a dozen clean empty egg shells into small pieces, two eggs at a time. In a small jar, mix three drop of blue food coloring with 2 T. water. Add 2 eggs shells, screw on lid, and shake gently for a minute or so until the shells turn blue. Drain and place on paper towel to dry. Repeat with other colors. Spread a thin layer of glue over a half-size piece of construction paper. Sprinkle each color of egg shells over it in either different colored lines, or mix them all together all over the paper. Let dry.

Suet Cakes

Make suet cakes to feed the birds. Mix melted suet or peanut butter with bird seed and pour into egg cartons. When hardened, the whole carton can be placed outside on a window sill or other ledge for the birds.

Jelly beans make fun eggs to eat. Use the cookie nests you saved from the previous day and put a few jelly "eggs" into each one.

Deviled eggs or just hard-boiled eggs are fun, too.

DAY 4
BIRDS IN OUR AREA

MATERIALS
Pictures of local birds
Finger Birds: colored
    construction paper
Snack: popcorn

PROJECTS
Cheerio Strings: Cheerios, string
Bird Mobile: pictures from Day 1, cardboard or poster board, general mobile
    materials
Bird Matching Game: bird stickers, cardboard or poster board

Show pictures of robins, sparrows, woodpeckers, blue jays, cardinals, etc.—the birds that live in your part of the country.

Birds get their names in many ways. Some are named because of their colors, such as the cardinal (red) and bluebird (blue). Others get their names from their cries, such as the whippoorwill. Others, from what they do: woodpeckers use their bills to peck into wood to find food; flycatchers catch insects while they are flying. Usually, the male birds have brighter colors than the females. The female birds can hide better in their nest, so their colors are not so bright.

Ask the child if he has ever seen any of these birds around the neighborhood. Some of these birds may already be coming to the food that you've put outside this week.

Fly, Homer, Fly, Bill Peet
Hi, Mr. Robin, Alvin Tresselt
Sammy, the Crow Who Remembered, Elizabeth Hazelton
Sparrow Socks, George Thompson
The Red Horse and the Bluebird, Sandy Rainowitz
The Restless Robin, Marjorie Flack
The Royal Raven, Hans Wilhelm

Finger Birds

Here is Mr. Bluebird—fly Mr. Bluebird
Here is Mr. Cardinal—fly Mr. Cardinal
Here is Mr. Oriole—fly Mr. Oriole
Here is Mr. Hummingbird—fly Mr. Hummingbird
Here is Mr. Blackbird—fly Mr. Blackbird
The birds fly and sing for now it is spring.

(Make a little colored bird as shown for each color. Tape to fingernails and wiggle that finger when you talk about it. Make one for your child's fingers—this is a good way to begin to teach colors).

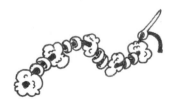

Cheerio Strings
String Cheerios and popcorn and hang in a tree for the birds.

Bird Mobile

Cut out the birds that were colored on Day 1, mount on cardboard or white poster board and make into a mobile.

Bird Matching Game

Using the directions in Chapter 2, make a bird matching game using songbird stickers.

Make popcorn. Have the child throw some out for the birds, after taking what he wants to eat.

DAY 5
BIRDS IN OTHER PARTS OF THE WORLD

MATERIALS
Pictures of birds found in other
  parts of the world
Snack: crackers with cheese
  or jelly

PROJECTS
Paper Pelican: white poster board, colored construction paper, glue or tape
Parrot or Penguin Puzzle: picture of bird, cardboard, glue

Show pictures of parrots, macaws, canaries, and other tropical birds. Talk about their brightly colored feathers and how they stand out against the dark foliage of the jungle. Have the child imagine what it would be like to be a parrot or a macaw living in the rain forest. What does he think that the bird does and sees all day?

Look at the beaks of these birds. let the child guess why their beaks are so big. Talk about the pelican and how his beak is like a giant scoop to gather fish in the water.

Talk about the kinds of food that these birds eat. Talk about the danger that they have from animals who might hurt them.

Repeat the above discussion with penguins, ostriches, etc.

But Where is the Green Parrot?, Thomas and Wanda Zacharias
Come Again, Pelican, Don Freeman
How the Ostrich Got Its Long Neck, Verna Aardema
I Met a Penguin, Frank Asch
Nanette the Hungry Pelican, William Wise
Percy the Parrot series, Wayne Carly
The Painter and the Bird, Max Velthuijs
The Peacock Who Lost His Tail, John Hamberger
The Spooky Tail of Prewit Peacock, Bill Peet
Tweedles Be Brave!, Wolo

A Funny Old Bird

A funny old bird is the pelican.   (shake finger)
His mouth   (point to mouth)
Can hold more than his belly can.   (point to stomach)

Parrot or Penguin Puzzle

Glue a picture of a parrot or penguin onto a piece of cardboard. Or, if you're artistic, draw one and have the child color it. Cut into pieces and have the child put the pieces back together.

Paper Pelican

Make a pelican with a pocket-pouch in which to put fish. Draw a pelican picture (as shown) onto white poster board, color and cut out. Draw a duplicate pattern of the pouch onto white construction paper. Glue or tape the sides and the bottom to the front side of the pouch forming a pocket. The fish are cut out of colored construction paper. They can be numbered and placed in the bill in numerical order to help the child learn to count, or they can be placed in by color to help the child learn his colors. The fish can also be made in various sizes and numbered to help the child learn about size as well. Adapt this to fit your child's age.

Field Trip to a Pet Store or Zoo

Visit a pet store or zoo and help the child identify the birds. Review their coloring, beaks, etc.

In keeping with "Polly Wants a Cracker," serve the child crackers (perhaps with jelly or cheese) as a treat.

DAY 6
BIRDS OF PREY

MATERIALS
Pictures of birds of prey

PROJECTS
Owl Puzzle: picture of owl, cardboard, glue

Show pictures of eagles, hawks, and owls. Talk about how these birds differ from the little birds that we normally see around us.

Explain how much bigger these birds are than the others we have talked about. These birds are hunting birds, since they eat small animals such as rabbits and mice, rather than berries or seeds. If your child expresses concern about this, you may want to explain that many animals eat other animals—we eat cattle, pigs, etc. This is all part of nature's plan to keep each species in balance with others.

Talk about an owl: how soft and furry its feathers look, how it sleeps during the daytime and hunts at night, how it can turn its head around on its neck to look in all directions, how its call sounds like "who, who."

Hawk, I'm Your Brother, Byrd Baylor
Moose, Michael Foreman
Orlando, the Brave Vulture, Tomi Ungerer
Tell Me, Mr. Owl, Doris Foster
The Happy Owls, Celestino Piatti
The Owl Who Hated the Dark, Earle Goodenow
The Wide-Awake Owl, Louis Slobodkin

The Owl Says Who

The owl by day can't see 'tis said.
Whoo, Whoo, Whoo.
He sits and blinks and turns his head.   (act out)
Whoo, Whoo, Whoo.
But when the stars come out at night,   (open and close hands
                                                                quickly like stars twinkling)
Whoo, Whoo, Whoo.
He calls his wife with all his might.   (put hands to mouth as though
                                                              calling someone)
Whoo, Whoo, Whoo.

The Wise Old Owl

A wise old owl sat in an oak.
The more he saw, the less he spoke.
The less he spoke, the more he heard.
Now why can't we be like that wise old bird?

Owl Puzzle

Make an owl puzzle by mounting an owl drawing or picture onto cardboard with glue or spray adhesive. Cut into pieces—the size and number will depend on the age of your child.

DAY 1	**TURKEYS**
DAY 2	**NATIVE AMERICANS**
DAY 3	**PILGRIMS AND THANKSGIVING**

In this chapter, the child will learn about turkeys. He will learn about Native Americans, the "Indians," who met the Pilgrims. He will learn about the Pilgrims, their reason for coming to America, and why we celebrate Thanksgiving. He will also learn about Thanksgiving, about being "thankful," and to think about the blessings he has.

MATERIALS

Picture of a turkey

PROJECTS

Construction Paper Turkeys: construction paper
Turkey Game: construction paper, glue, tape
Mosaic Turkey: cardboard, marker, fillers such as beans, popcorn,
  dried peas, buttons

Show a picture of a turkey and have the child identify it. Help him
understand what makes it different from other birds—its fan-shaped tail,
the way it struts around, its size, the size and color of its head, and its
call, "gobble, gobble."

Tell him that the turkey is one of the symbols of Thanksgiving.

Sometimes It's Turkeys, Sometimes It's Feathers, Lorna Balian
Turkeys, Pilgrims, and Indian Corn, Edna Barth

My children love this story of the turkey with the terrible temper. The
story is especially fun to tell if you cut out eight colored turkeys: brown,
red, blue, purple, green, yellow, white, and pink, plus single feathers in
all colors but brown. You may want to write the verses on the backs of
the turkeys, so you can just about tell the story without reading it. Put
tacky glue or tape on the backs of the feathers, so they can be attached to
the brown turkey as you go along.

Tommy was a turkey with a terrible temper. He was a brown turkey who
often flew around screaming and yelling.

One day, he lost his temper over some little thing and turned as red as a
beet (hold up red turkey). The other turkeys laughed and said:

> "You're red, red, red, red, as a beet,
> Red from your head to the tip of your feet."

Tommy ran away and hid for a long time. When he calmed down, he
realized he was still red all over. He ran to wise Dr. Owl to ask him what
to do.

"You must learn to control that terrible temper of yours, or you will be
very sorry," hooted wise Dr. Owl. "That is all I can say, but come back to
me in a week."

The next morning, Tommy was brown again except for a red feather in his tail (glue red feather to brown turkey).

Tommy's mother called him to come help with the Monday wash, but he got the blues as soon as he had to start working. He groaned and moaned until Mother finally told him he was acting like a baby. You can guess what happened next—he lost his temper again. This time, though, he turned <u>blue</u> all over (hold up blue turkey).

As he was running away to hide, the other turkeys yelled:

> "You're blue, blue from your head to your toe.
> Blue all over wherever you go."

This time, Tommy blamed his mother for causing him to lose his temper. The next morning, he was a brown turkey again, except for the blue feather next to the red one in his tail (glue blue feather to brown turkey).

You can guess what happened the rest of the week. On Tuesday, Tommy didn't want to help clean up the yard. He said he hated cleaning with a purple passion. Soon, he had turned purple all over (hold up purple turkey).

The turkeys all shouted:

> "You're purple, purple, that's all we can see;
> You'd better go hide yourself under a tree."

Of course, Tommy sat and blamed everything on everyone else. On Wednesday morning, he was a brown turkey again, but he had a purple feather along with the red and blue ones (glue purple feather to brown turkey).

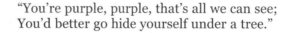

He went out for a walk and saw a turkey friend eating a big ear of corn. Tommy was green with envy, because he didn't have one. Before he knew it, he was in a terrible temper tantrum and was green all over (hold up green turkey).

The turkeys turned on him again and yelled:

> "You're green, green, green as grass.
> Why don't you get wise and stop all your sass."

Tommy again went back to his hiding place and started feeling sorry for himself.

The next day, he was brown, but now he had a green feather among the other brightly-colored tail feathers (glue green feather to brown turkey). But something was happening to Tommy. He was beginning to really want to change. He wanted to keep his temper and decided to try harder.

Of course, all the turkeys liked to tease Tommy. During a game the turkeys were playing, they called Tommy a coward. The turkeys also said he had a yellow streak down his back. Before he could think, Tommy was having another temper tantrum and turned yellow (hold up yellow turkey).

They yelled:

"You're yellow, yellow just like we said.
Why don't you go home and hide under your bed."

This time, Tommy sat under the tree and thought a long time about everything. He realized he was really the only one who could make things better.

The next day, with his new yellow feather, he decided to really try to change (glue yellow feather to brown turkey). Mother asked him to watch the baby turkeys while she went shopping. When they ran through the house with muddy feet, Tommy almost lost his temper. He tried so hard not to lose his temper that he turned white (hold up white turkey).

The other turkeys shouted:

"You're white, white but your temper didn't show.
Maybe you're changing, we really hope so."

The next day, Tom was proud to have that white feather (glue on white feather). All day, Saturday and Sunday, he kept calm without a single tantrum, and he was tickled pink (add a pink feather to the brown turkey).

On Monday, he went back to Dr. Owl and thanked him for his help. Dr. Owl told Tommy that he could wear his beautiful tail proudly now.

So, if you ever see a turkey with his tail unfolded, strutting around, remember this story of the turkey with the terrible temper.

Target Turkey

Make a turkey picture by cutting out circles of various colors: one each—7", 6½", 4", 2½". Glue on top of each other, adding a brown head and feet. This can be used to make a "Pin the Head on the Turkey" game with tape on the heads to secure them to the turkey.

Mosaic Turkey

Make a mosaic turkey picture by tracing an outline of the child's hand onto a heavy piece of paper or cardboard. The inside can be filled with beans, yarn, string, buttons, seeds, cloth, etc. (This can also just be colored in if the child is too young to handle the beans, etc.)

Prepare frozen or canned corn. The child can pretend to be a turkey while he eats the corn.

Turkey noodle soup.

Cup Cake Turkeys

Bake cup cakes. Cool. If you used paper liners, these should be removed. Turn cupcakes upside down on plate and frost pale brown. (This color can be made by mixing cocoa into white frosting until desired color is reached). Cut a tail out of orange construction paper. Insert into back of cupcake. Cut head of brown construction paper. Color in eyes, beak, etc., and insert into the front of the cupcake.

DAY 2
NATIVE AMERICANS

MATERIALS
Pictures of Native Americans

PROJECTS
Headband: construction paper, feathers, either real or cut from paper, stapler
Vest: large paper grocery bag, crayons or markers
Drum: empty oatmeal box, brown construction paper, crayons or markers
Necklace: wooden beads or macaroni (you will need food coloring if you use this), yarn or string
Teepee: construction paper, glue or tape, crayons

The Native Americans lived here for many hundreds of years before any white people came to live in America. The Native Americans were very important to the early settlers in America, because they taught them how to hunt for wild turkey, plant corn and use dead fish for fertilizer.

Through the years, the Native Americans have been taken advantage of and looked down upon. They had a rich cultural heritage of their own which the white people didn't understand. Today, we say "Native Americans" rather than Indians which means that they lived here first.

Talk about the kinds of clothes Native Americans wore when they were first found here. Explain that they dress just like us now, except when they have special ceremonies or activities.

Talk about what kind of food they ate and how they found food. They planted corn and ground it into maize flour. They hunted for wild animals, such as deer and buffalo, and caught fish. They also ate berries and roots.

Indian Two Feet and the ABC Moose Hunt, Margaret Friskey
Little Chief, Syd Hoff
Little Indian, Peggy Parish
Little Owl Indian, Hetty Beatty
Little Sky Eagle and the Pumpkin Drum, Mildred H. Feague
Navaho Pet, Patricia M. Martin
Navaho Stories, Edward Dolch
One Little Indian Boy, Emma Brock
When Clay Sings, Byrd Baylor

Headband

Cut a 2" strip of paper the width of the child's head. Have him decorate it with crayons or markers. Then staple or tape the ends together. Feathers can be cut from paper, too, or real ones can be purchased at a craft store.

Vest

Simple copies of traditional Native American costumes are easy to make out of a brown grocery bags. Slit an opening up the middle of the front of the bag. Cut holes in the top and sides for his arms and neck. Draw designs on it with crayons or markers. A few streaks of rouge or eye shadow across the child's nose and cheeks will complete the picture.

Drum

An empty oatmeal box makes a perfect drum. Cover the sides with brown construction paper and decorate again with crayons or markers.

Teepees

Out of construction paper, cut out a circle the size that you would like the teepee. Slit up one side to the center. Have the child color designs around the edge. Overlap sides of slit and glue or tape. A flap opening can be added, too, by cutting a small slit and folding back the edge.

Necklace

A necklace can be made from colored macaroni. In an empty glass jar, mix ¼ c. colored water to 1 c. dry macaroni. Repeat with different colors. When it's the color you desire, drain and dry on waxed paper or paper towels overnight. Wooden beads can also be purchased from a craft store. Have the child push yarn or string through the openings. The yarn is easier to thread if you wrap the end with cellophane tape.

Any recipe using corn is appropriate. Here is one we like for Native American Corn Cakes:

1 ¼ c. cornmeal	1 ¼ c. milk
6 T. flour	1 egg, slightly beaten
2 tsp. baking powder	3 T. oil
½ tsp. salt	

Combine first four ingredients. Add wet ingredients. Mix into a thin batter as for pancakes. Use about 2 T. for each cake. Fry on a greased griddle. Serve with butter and jam. Makes about 15.

DAY 3
PILGRIMS AND THANKSGIVING

MATERIALS
Pilgrim pictures

PROJECTS
Paper Bag Pilgrims: lunch bags, black tempera paint, newspaper, glue
Pilgrim Hats: 18" x 24" pieces of black and white construction paper, stapler, glue

Begin by telling the story of the Pilgrims and why they were thankful:

Many, many years ago, a small ship came to America. It was called the Mayflower. The people on the ship were called Pilgrims. They didn't have electricity, grocery stores, telephones, cars, or running water. They wore different clothing than we do today. They came to America to worship God as they wanted.

It took them two months to come to America. When they finally arrived, it was December. It was very cold, and they didn't have very much food. There were no homes waiting for them (if you live in a climate that gets cold in the winter, ask the child how he would like to have to sleep out at night in a tent instead of in his nice, warm house).

The Native Americans already lived in America. They made friends with the Pilgrims and taught them how to build homes and hunt for food.

In the spring, the weather became warm again. The Pilgrims were happy and went to work right away. They plowed the land. They planted the seeds they had brought from England.

The sun shone all summer long. The rain watered the plants. When fall came, the Pilgrims gathered all the fruits and vegetables they had planted. They stored them away for winter.

Everyone was happy. The Pilgrims decided to have a big feast to thank God for their food and for all of their blessings. They decided to invite all their Native American friends.

On the day of the feast, the Native Americans brought wild turkeys they had shot with their bows and arrows. The Pilgrims covered the tables with all the good things they had grown in their gardens. Before anyone ate, they bowed their heads and thanked God for all their many blessings. This was the very first Thanksgiving.

Talk about all the things for which the child has to be thankful for. Help him understand that on Thanksgiving Day, we shouldn't just think about all the good things to eat, but also about the many blessings we have received during the past year.

Arthur's Thanksgiving, Marc Brown
Cranberry Thanksgiving, Wende and Harry Devlin
Fried Feathers for Thanksgiving, James Stevenson
Little Bear's Thanksgiving, Janice
Miranda's Pilgrims, Rosemary Well
Over the River and Through the Woods, Lydia M. Child
The Plymouth Thanksgiving, Leonard Weisgard (this story might be
      too difficult for a child to understand, but the illustrations
      are wonderful)
The Thanksgiving Story, Alice Dalgliesh
Things to Make and Do For Thanksgiving, Lovinda Cauley

Five Little Pilgrims

Five little Pilgrims on Thanksgiving Day.
The first one said, "I'll have potatoes, if I may."
The second one said, "I'll have turkey roasted."
The third one said, "I'll have chestnuts toasted."
The fourth one said, "Oh, cranberries I spy."
The fifth one said, "I'll have some pumpkin pie."
(Hold up a finger as you talk about each Pilgrim)

Over the River

Over the river and through the woods
To Grandmother's house we go.
The horse knows the way to carry the sleigh
Through the white and drifted snow.
Over the river and through the woods,
Oh, how the wind does blow.
It stings our nose and bites our toes,
As over the ground it goes.

Over the river and through the woods
And right through the barnyard gate.
We seem to go extremely slow,
And I can hardly wait.
Over the river and through the woods.
Now grandmother's cap I spy.
Hurrah for the fun! Is the pudding done?
Hurrah for the pumpkin pie!

Paper Bag Pilgrims

Make paper bag Pilgrims to decorate the Thanksgiving table. On a lunch
bag, paint a black belt and buttons. Stuff with newspaper as shown. Fold
top edge over and glue down (this will be the shoulders). Add a head,
arms, and feet.

Pilgrim Hats

Children love making Pilgrim hats—your child will probably want to wear one on Thanksgiving Day, too. You will need extra large sheets (use either 18" x 24" paper or two smaller pieces taped together) of white and black construction paper.

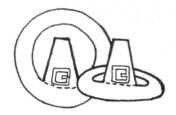

The boy's hat is an 11 ½" diameter circle. Use a compass or large plate to trace this. A 6 ½" diameter circle is traced inside, but only small sections are cut out, as shown. A white or yellow buckle piece can be glued on the cone-shaped piece.

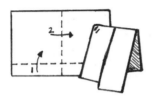

The girl's hat is a rectangle 18" x 12". Fold over one long end 4". Then fold the whole hat in half and staple several times in the bottom corner.

Have a mini-Thanksgiving. This can be a snack or lunch depending upon how elaborate you want to make it. Suggestions for food:

> Turkey luncheon meat
> Cranberry sauce
> Stove-Top™ stuffing
> Turkey noodle soup
> Corn or cornbread

December is a special time of year, no matter what your traditions. Our family separates discussions of Santa Claus from the birth of the Christ Child. The best friend of one of my sons is Jewish, and they celebrate Hanukkah. Kwanzaa is an African-American celebration. This chapter can be used with a single celebration, omitting the others, or all three can be covered. Candles and gifts are a part of all three celebrations and can be adapted for each one. We always try to spend several days celebrating traditions of others, because I think they broaden the child's viewpoint. Choose what works out best for you. Just remember to keep the whole month simple and don't wear yourself out!! There is so much excitement in the air that the child doesn't need a lot to keep him pretty keyed up. Happy Holidays!

DAY 1
WHAT IS CHRISTMAS?

MATERIALS
Pictures or drawings of
   Christmas symbols
Snack

PROJECTS
Advent Chain: red and green construction paper, glue

Ask the child what special time is coming? (Christmas). Tell him that this is a joyous time of year when we show our love for one another by exchanging gifts and doing nice things for other people.

Show him pictures or drawings of Christmas symbols. Help him learn what they are. Suggestions: star, wreath, candy canes, sleigh, bells, stocking, mistletoe, holly, poinsettia, etc.

9 Days to Christmas, Marie Hall Ets
Christmas Eve, Edith Hurd
Christmas, Dick Bruna
Counting the Days, James Sterling Tippett
It's Christmas, Gladys Adshead
Little Bear's Christmas, Janice
The Christmas Party, Adrienne Adams
Twelve Days of Christmas, Jack Kent

Jingle Bells

Jingle bells, jingle bells,
Jingle all the way.
Oh, what fun it is to ride
In a one-horse open sleigh.
Jingle bells, jingle bells,
Jingle all the way.
Oh what fun it is to ride
In a one horse open sleigh.

If you have some bells, the child can shake them while the song is being sung.

Advent Chain

Have the child make a paper chain, using alternating green and red strips of paper. Make the same number of rings as the days until Christmas. Attach to a 6" star, bell, or tree cut out of colored construction paper. Hang up and let the child tear off one chain each day. (This saves a lot of questions about how soon Christmas will be here!)

Make Christmas cookies (recipe in Appendix).

DAY 2
CHRISTMAS TREES

MATERIALS
Picture of a pine tree and a
   Christmas tree
Snack

PROJECTS
Stand-Up Tree: green poster board, multi-colored star stickers, multi-colored
   paper punch circles

Tree Mobile: green construction paper, glitter, sequins, glue (see general
   directions in Chapter 2)

Animal Christmas Tree: popcorn, peanut butter, pine cones, bread, orange
   halves, paper cups with nuts and seeds, carrots

Show a picture of a pine tree. Ask the child what it is. Show a picture of a
Christmas tree. Ask the child what this is. Talk about how they are
different.

Discuss how people get their Christmas trees. Some people buy one from
a Christmas tree lot in the city; some go out in the forest and cut down
their own tree. Others don't have a real tree at all, but use an artificial
one. Some families decorate their tree early in December, and others
wait until Christmas Eve.

There are many decorations for a Christmas tree. In America, we hang
strings of colored lights, but in many countries, the tree is lit with little
candles.

Christmas Tree on the Mountain, Carol Fenner
Mr. Willowby's Christmas Tree, Robert Barry
The Beautiful Christmas Tree, Charlotte Zolotow
The Biggest Christmas Tree on Earth, Fernando Krahn
The Bird's Christmas Tree, Emma Brock
The Little Fir Tree, Margaret Brown
The Silver Christmas Tree, Pat Hutchins

Stand-Up Trees

Cut two identical trees out of green poster board as shown. Cut a slit up
halfway in one and down halfway in the other. Join the two. They can be
decorated with star stickers and colored construction paper circles cut
with a paper punch. These are nice grouped together in different sizes.

Tree Mobile

Cut out trees from green construction paper. Decorate with glitter and
sequins. Hang from a mobile (see general directions in Chapter 2), so
they can twirl and catch the light.

Christmas Tree for the Animals

Decorate a tree outside for the animals. String popcorn. Dip pine cones in peanut butter and hang them on the tree with yarn. Poke orange halves onto strong branches. Hang paper cups from branches—fill with nuts or bird seed. Hang carrots down from low branches with string. (If you live in an apartment, you can hang these on your balcony).

Using a tree cookie cutter, cut slices of bread and make into sandwiches.

DAY 3
SANTA CLAUS

MATERIALS

Picture of Santa Claus
Reindeer Sandwich Snack: bread,
peanut butter, stick pretzels,
maraschino cherries, raisins

PROJECTS

Santa Picture: white paper, crayons, cotton balls, glue
Dancing Santa: white poster board, crayons, paper fasteners

Show a picture of Santa Claus. Ask who it is. (In our family, we don't put a lot of emphasis on Santa. We talk about him as a man who represents the spirit of love and giving at Christmas time. We never threaten the child to be good or Santa won't bring them any presents. Again, handle this however you want to.)

Many parents wonder whether it's lying to tell a child that there is a Santa Claus. From things we've read and from our own experience, we've decided that it's all right for the child to use their imaginations to pretend that Santa Claus, fairies, and elves really live. But we talk about Santa as someone who helps parents know what children would like for Christmas, and who makes the time of year more fun.

Describe the clothes Santa wears: his cap, his red suit, his black belt, and his black boots. Ask the child what they think his big fluffy beard must feel like.
Talk about the magical reindeer who pull the sleigh, the elves who help Santa in his shop at the North Pole, and the department store Santas— "Santa's helpers," as we call them—who help Santa talk to all the boys and girls.

Babar and Father Christmas, Jean de Brunhoff
Father Christmas, Raymond Briggs
How Mrs. Santa Saved Christmas, Phyllis P. McGinley
Rudolph the Red-Nosed Reindeer, Robert May
Santa's Moose, Syd Hoff
Santaberry and the Snard, Jack and Alice Schick

Santa Picture

Copy a large picture of Santa's face onto a piece of white paper (a coloring book is a good source). Have the child color it. Then have him glue cotton balls to make the beard and decorate his cap.

Dancing Santa

Outline a dancing Santa onto white construction paper as shown. Help the child color and cut out the pieces. Loosely attach together with yarn or paper fasteners. When the child holds onto his head and moves it up and down, Santa will "dance."

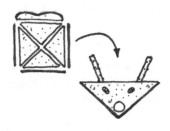

Reindeer Sandwich

Spread peanut butter on a slice of bread and cut diagonally to make four triangles. Place the point of each sandwich down and put two pretzel sticks in the flat top for antlers. Cut raisins in half to make eyes and a nose (or use a cherry cut in quarters to make "Rudolph.")

MATERIALS

Christmas symbols shown
in Day 1

PROJECTS

Paper Chains: red and green construction paper, glue
Sparkling Ornaments: pine cones, glitter or sequins, ribbon or yarn, glue
Bells: paper nut cups or egg carton cups, aluminum or colored foil, ribbon
Soldier Clothespins: old-fashioned wooden clothespins; red, pink, and black
acrylic paint; green pompon; ribbon; glue
Drums: 6-oz. orange juice cans with plastic strips, gold spray paint, wide red
ribbon, glue, gold cording, straight pins
Clothespin Reindeer: wooden clothespins, glue, wiggly eyes, small red pompons
for nose, brown yarn, black paint or marker, ribbon or cording for hanging

Again, talk about some of the Christmas symbols mentioned on Day 1:
star, bell, holly, tree, etc. Ask the child if he has seen any of these things
this month. Perhaps he will name others as well.

Tell him that the decorations add to the excitement of Christmas.
Explain that he's going to help you make some decorations for your
home today. Again, here are just a few suggestions:

Paper Chains

Make red and green paper chains to decorate the tree or perhaps his
bedroom.

Bells

These can be made from paper nut cups or the individual sections of egg
cartons. Cover with aluminum foil or other colored foil paper. Poke a
small hole in the top. Run a piece of ribbon through to hang. These are
also pretty using several different lengths of ribbon, hanging in a group
from a light fixture.

Sparkling Pine Cones

Roll pine cones in glue and then in glitter or sequins. Tie to the Christmas tree with ribbon or yarn.

Soldier Clothespins

Use old-fashioned wooden clothespins (not the spring type) and acrylics. You will want to have already painted the middle of the pin red for the jacket and the two "legs" black. Have the child dip the top part in pink paint for the face. When dry, he can glue on a bright green pompom hat. You can add facial features with a fine-tip pen and a ribbon to hang from the tree.

Drums

Use a clean 6-oz. orange juice can with lid (the kind with the plastic strip to release the lid, so it can be reattached). Spray gold paint on the lid and the bottom of the can. Cut the sides down to three inches high. Glue on wide red ribbon. Glue gold cording on in a diagonal pattern. Glue top lid back on and add a gold cord to hang from the tree.

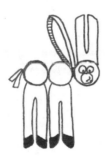

Clothespin Reindeer

Glue two old-fashioned clothespins together to form legs as shown. Glue a third clothespin going up instead of down. After clothespins dry, glue on wiggly eyes, a red pompom nose and two pieces of brown yarn for the tail. The hooves can be painted black or colored with a black marker. Tie a piece of cording or ribbon around neck for hanging.

DAY 5
CHRISTMAS IN OTHER LANDS

We like to take several days to talk about Christmas in other lands. There are many resource books at your library with detailed information about Christmas around the world. Here are some of our favorite activities from a number of countries (you can decide the amount of time you want to spend). The projects and materials needed will depend on the countries and activities you choose.

9 Days to Christmas, Marie Hall Ets
An Edwardian Christmas, John S. Goodall
An English Christmas, Celia McInnes
Baboushka and the Three Kings, Ruth Robbins
Christmas in Germany, Passport Books
Christmas in the Stable, Astrid Lindgren
Christmas Trolls, Jan Brett
Din Dan Don, It's Christmas, Janina Domanska
Father Christmas, Raymond Briggs
Joy Through the World, Allen D. Bragdon
Merry Christmas, Strega Nona, Tomie de Paola
Noel for Jeanne-Marie, Francoise Segnolose
Plum Pudding for Christmas, Virginia Kahl
The Christmas Pinata, Jack Kent
Twelve Days of Christmas, illustrated by Susan Swan

Mexico

A bright pinata is part of the Mexican Christmas. We begin this several days in advance of our Mexican day. Blow up a large balloon and tie. Mix ¼ c. cornstarch, 2 c. water, and ½ c. flour in a large bowl. One by one, dip newspaper strips into the mixture and cover the balloon until there are three layers of paper. Let dry at least a day on a cookie rack or hang from the balloon stem, so that all the surfaces can dry thoroughly. Then paint and decorate it, and fill it with candy. This night we go around caroling to our neighbors and friends (our own version of the Mexican posada), and return home for enchiladas and the breaking of the pinata.

Scandinavian Countries

One morning before Christmas, our daughter, singing Christmas carols, takes a plate of Christmas rolls and a mug of hot chocolate to each family member in his or her bed. She is the Lucia Girl. (I'm sure you can use a boy, if you don't have a girl) We usually have a smorgasbord for dinner that night that the preschoolers help prepare that day. Our smorgasbord is made up of different small dishes of food that we serve buffet style.

The Lucia Girl or Queen is the tradition in **Sweden**. Lucia was a beautiful Christian maiden who lived many years ago in Italy. Because she refused to give up her religion, she was burned at the stake. She was made a saint. Now one knows why she became so popular in Sweden. Her saint's day falls on December 13th, a day that was celebrated in pre-Christian Sweden as the beginning of the Festival of Light or Winter

Solstice. Today in Sweden, the youngest daughter is the Lucia Queen. She dresses in white with a ring of lighted candles on her head. (We use a ring of gold tinsel).

In **Norway**, the people remember the animals and birds at Christmas. You can use the ideas in Chapter 7, Birds.

For dessert, we make the traditional **Danish** rice porridge.

1 c. water	2 tsp. vanilla
1 ½ c. rice	1 T. almond extract
1 quart milk	½ pint whipped cream
2 T. sugar	1 or 2 whole almonds

Boil water and rice for two minutes. Stir in milk and cook at low heat for approximately 30 minutes. Add sugar, vanilla, and almond extract. When rice mixture is cold, fold in whipped cream and almonds. You can serve this with cherry pie filling.

England

In England, an immense Yule log is pulled into the house by the family. We celebrate with our log about the middle of the month. We follow their custom of using a piece of the log left from the year before to light the new log. This is supposed to bring luck in the coming year. We go caroling this night and come home for wassail or hot chocolate.

Mistletoe was believed by the ancient inhabitants of Britain, the Celtic Druids, to protect against evil and bring good luck. This was used in early Christmas celebrations before the Christmas tree. The "Kissing Bough" or "Kissing Ring" was suspended from the ceiling with mistletoe hanging from it. It was said that a kiss given under the mistletoe was a pledge of friendship and good will.

A **Kissing Ring** can be made by bending two wire coat hangers in circles, matching up the two hooks. Use fine wire to attach the hangers together at the bottom and top to form a circle. Christmas ribbon can be wrapped around the frame. You can also add short pieces of real or silk evergreens. Tie a bunch of mistletoe to the bottom with a ribbon. Tie a ribbon to the top of the frame as well.

When my parents were in England, they sent us our first box of Christmas crackers. These are cardboard tubes, filled with a paper crown, a wish, and a small trinket, such as a whistle or tiny top. When the strings or paper pulls on the outside are tugged sharply, the cracker "bangs" and the prizes are removed. We purchase these every year now and they are a part of our Christmas Eve buffet dinner.

Germany

In Germany the advent wreath is an important part of the Christmas season. Four Sundays before Christmas, we put out our wreath. Three of the colors are the same and one is a lighter color. We light the first candle that night, sing carols, and read some of the Christmas story from the Bible. One Sunday later, we light two candles, read, and sing. The third Sunday we light the candle that is lighter along with the previous two. The fourth Sunday, all are lit.

"Away in a Manger," "Silent Night," "Hark the Herald Angels Sing," and "O Tannenbaum" are four familiar hymns from Germany, so we sing them when we light our wreath.

An easy **advent wreath** can be made as follows:

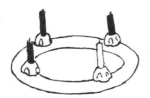

Cut out four cups from an egg carton. Cut holes out of the bottom the same size as your candles and place them inside. Attach with tape or a glue gun to a Styrofoam® circle (the size is determined by you). Cut real or silk evergreen branches into small sprays and stick in the Styrofoam® to completely cover the ring. Ribbon bows and pinecones can be added if desired.

In keeping with the advent concept, we have purchased advent calendars for the children to open each day before Christmas.

We also like to make gingerbread houses. In recent years, we have made these from graham crackers "glued" with frosting to an empty ½ pt. milk or whipped cream carton. We decorate these with small candies, M & M's, and little candy canes.

Other days can be spent making Christmas cookies, breads, or holiday food from other lands.

DAY 6
WHAT IS HANUKKAH?

MATERIALS
Snack

PROJECTS
Hanukkah Puppets: paper lunch bags, colored construction paper, scissors, glue

We tell a simplified version of the story of this celebration. Over 2,000 years ago, with a man named Judah Maccabee as their leader, the Jewish people rebelled against some wicked men who would not let them practice their religion. After the Jews won the war, they returned to Jerusalem and found that their temple was badly damaged. Soon they had cleaned it up and planned to relight the great menorah or candleholder. The only holy oil found was enough for one day. By a miracle, it burned for eight days.

It is to remember this great event that Jews celebrate for eight days each year. Hanukkah usually falls during the month of December. A new candle is lit each night for eight nights until all are lit on the final night. In Israel, all the school are closed and businesses are shut down. For eight nights there are lights shining from all the windows of the homes.

Jewish children are given gifts and money called "gelt." They are usually asked to give part of this money to the needy.

A favorite game to play at Hanukkah is the spinning of the dreidel, a four-sided top. The signs on the four sides stand for "A Great Miracle Happened Over There."

It would be interesting for the child to hear how his grandparents or other older friends celebrated Hanukkah when they were young.

A Hanukkah for Dina, Floreva Cohen
Did Judah Maccabee Water Ski?, Sol Scharfstein
Happy Hanukkah, Everybody, Hyman and Alice Chanover
I Love Hanukkah, Marilyn Hirsch
It's Chanukah, Ellie Gellman
Light the Lights, Margaret Moorman (an excellent story of how one
      family celebrates both Hanukkah and Christmas)
My First Hanukkah Book, Aileen Fisher
My Very Own Chanukah, Judith Saypol and Madeline Wikler
Peanut Butter, Jelly and Latkes, Sol Scharfstein
Potato Pancakes All Around, Marilyn Hirsch
The First Book of Chanukah, Robert Sol
The Hanukkah Book, Merilyn Burns
The Power of Light (8 stories for Hanukkah), Isaac Singer

Hanukkah Puppets

On the flap of a paper bag, glue colored shapes to look like hair, eyes, and a nose. Glue a small strip of red paper under the flap to be the mouth. Cut out arms and paste them on the sides of the bag. Glue a sword in one hand and a shield in the other hand of the puppet to be Judah Maccabee. Other puppets can be Hannah, her seven sons, and Eliezer the Priest.

The Jewish people eat food that is cooked in oil, such as fried donuts, to symbolize victory. Roast goose is often eaten. Cookies in the shapes of candles, the Star of David, dreidels, and elephants (symbolizing the Syrian Way Elephant), and menorahs are baked and enjoyed. One favorite recipe:

Potato Latkes

> 6 medium potatoes, peeled and shredded
> 1 medium onion, coarsely shredded
> 2 eggs
> 3 T. flour
> 1½ tsp. salt
> ¼ tsp. pepper

In a large bowl, mix potatoes, onion, eggs, flour, salt and pepper. In large frying pan, heat enough oil to coat bottom. Drop batter by ¼ c. into oil. With back of spoon spread evenly to 3" pancakes. Cook over medium heat until golden brown and crisp, turning once. Drain on paper towels. Place on warm platter, garnish with parsley. Serve with applesauce, sour cream and/or preserves.

DAY 7
MENORAHS

MATERIALS
Picture of a menorah: colored
  construction paper, scissors,
  glue or stapler, tape
Snack

PROJECTS
Egg Carton Menorah: empty egg carton, paint or markers, clay
Spool Menorah: nine empty wooden spools, paint or markers
Paper Chain Menorah: construction paper, glue or tape
Cardboard Menorah: empty paper towel roll, Popsicle® sticks, yellow tissue
  paper, glue, paper cup

Show a picture of a menorah. Explain that this is a very special candle-stick which holds nine candles. The candle in the middle is called the "shammash" which means "servant," and it is used to light the other candles. It stands either higher or lower than the other candles.

Each night for eight nights a new candle is lit and then any old candles are relit. Special prayers are said in English or Hebrew. The menorah is always lit after sunset and is placed in a window.

There are no special designs, so you can use any holders that you wish.

Light Another Candle: The Story and Meaning of Hanukkah, Miriam Chaikin

Other Hannukah books listed in Day 6.

Egg Carton Menorah

Cut three compartments from an egg carton so there are nine holes and paint it any color that you wish. The sides can be decorated with dreidels or Stars of David. Put a piece of clay in each carton to set the candles each evening before lighting.

Spool Menorah

Using 9 empty wooden spools (available at craft stores), paint and decorate as shown. Place a candle in the spools each evening.

Paper Chain Menorah

Staple or glue strips of colored paper together in rings to form long chains. Tape one long chain for the shammash and stand to a window or wall. Tape smaller chains as illustrated to represent the eight candle holders.

Cardboard Menorah

Cut nine slits across the top of a cardboard tube, such as from an empty paper towel, a wrapping paper roll or a mailing tube. Glue the tube to an inverted paper cup to stabilize. Decorate. Paint ten Popsicle® sticks. Glue two together to make the tall shammash (the center candle used to light the others each night.) Paste yellow tissue paper to the top of each stick for flames. Place the shammash in the menorah and add one candle each night of Hanukkah.

Eat any of the suggested foods in Day 6.

MATERIALS

PROJECTS
Cardboard Dreidel: cardboard, marker, pencil
Dreidel Cube: cardstock, marker, glue or tape

Nun   Gimmel   Hey   Shin

Dreidel, which is a special Hanukkah game, is played using a special top, also called a dreidel. It can be purchased at a Jewish gift shop, a card shop during December or one can be made. The game is played using beans, pennies, or chips. Each person puts one item into the middle. The first person spins the top and receives the reward that appears on the side: Nun—take nothing, Gimmel—take everything, Hey—take half the pot, and Shin—put one back. The one with the most at the end is the winner and will win a prize of gelt (money).

The Dreidel Book, Sol Scharfstein

Other Hanukkah books listed in Day 6

Dreidel Song (music in Appendix)

My dreidel, dreidel, dreidel
I made it out of clay.
My dreidel, dreidel, dreidel
My dreidel I will play.

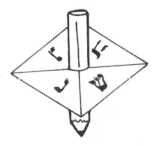

Cardboard Dreidel

Cut a 2 or 3 inch cardboard square. Draw lines from corner to corner to divide it diagonally. Draw the symbols in each section. Cut a hole through the center and insert a pencil through the hole until it will spin easily.

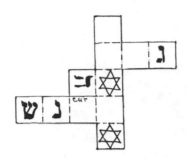

Dreidel Cube

Make a pattern as shown enlarging the squares to at least 1". Cut out and fold or cut as shown. Glue ends together to make a cube. This can be thrown like a die to play the dreidel game.

Dreidel Sandwiches

Cut a piece of cheese in the shape of a dreidel. Put on a piece of bread. Melt in the oven or microwave. Before serving, draw one of the dreidel signs on with ketchup as shown.

DAY 9
WHAT IS KWANZAA?

MATERIALS
Bright placemat, ears of corn, fruits and vegetables
Snack

PROJECTS
Kinara Candleholder: see candleholder ideas in Day 7
Beaded Necklace: large plastic beads, bright shoelace

Kwanzaa is a seven-day celebration that begins the day after Christmas and goes until New Year's Day. It was started in 1966 to help African-Americans remember their heritage. It is not a religious celebration, so it doesn't matter what your beliefs are to celebrate it.

Kwanzaa means "first fruits." The people get together and celebrate the good crops and harvest just as their ancestors did. This is a good time to talk about the past year and the things that you have been able to accomplish. Each day, a different principle is talked about. These are unity, self-determination, collective work and responsibility, cooperative economics, purpose, creativity, and faith.

A brightly woven straw place mat called a Mkeka (pronounced em-KAY-kah) is placed on the table representing tradition. One ear of corn is placed on the mat for each child in the family. You can also add other vegetables and fruits to represent the harvest. This is similar to the cornucopia at Thanksgiving.

One of the important aspects of Kwanzaa as in Hanukkah is the nightly lighting of candles. Seven candles are used in a Kinara candleholder that symbolizes the continent of Africa and its people. A black candle stands in the middle to symbolize the black people. The three candles on the right are green and symbolize the future. The three candles on the left are red and symbolize struggle. The candles are lit in the order shown below:

> The first day the black candle (Umoja) is lit.
> Day 2 symbolizes Self-determination (Kujichagulia).
> Day 3 symbolizes Collective work and responsibility (Ujima).
> Day 4 symbolizes Cooperative economics (Ujamaa).
> Day 5 symbolizes Purpose (Nia).
> Day 6 symbolizes Creativity (Kuumba).
> Day 7 symbolizes Faith (Imani).

The Karamu feast is traditionally held on the night of Kuumba (creativity), Dec. 31, the sixth day of Kwanzaa. This night is special because it is the end of the old year. The people try to wear clothing that is African just as their ancestors wore. They wear beaded necklaces, and the girls wear "bubas" which are an African dress. The boys wear "kanzus."

Part of the evening involves lighting the kinara before the meal. This night can be celebrated by just the family, or with other invited friends and relatives. At the beginning of the evening, each person pours water into the soil (you can use a potted plant) as they mention the name of an ancestor. After each name, everyone says achê (ah-shay) which means "so let it be." They play games and dance. They also exchange gifts.

On this night, the children in the family talk about what they have accomplished during the past year and their hopes and dreams for the future.

Kwanzaa, Deborah M. Newton Chocolate
Kwanzaa: Everything You Always Wanted to Know But Didn't Know Where to Ask, Cedric McClester
Seven Candles for Kwanzaa, Andrea Davis Pinkney (this is a great book explaining this celebration to children)

Kinara (Kwanzaa Candleholder)
Use any of the ideas in Day 8, Menorahs, substituting 7 holders for the 9 used in Hanukkah.

Beaded Necklaces

Using large plastic beads available at craft stores and a bright colored shoelace at least 20" long, a child can string a necklace for himself. Tie a loose knot in one end of the lace until all the beads are on. Then untie and put around the child's neck. Tie the ends securely, allowing enough room so that the necklace can slip over the child's head. If the child is too young to manipulate the beads through the shoelace, have him pick out the colors that he wants and you can do the beading. This is also a good way to reinforce his understanding of colors.

Gifts

Kwanzaa gifts, made by hand, are called zawadi. The gifts listed in Day 11 can be made by the child for Kwanzaa. Grownups give gifts to children to reward them for the promises they've made and kept throughout the year.

The child can help prepare the food for the feast (Karamu). The food you choose to serve should be healthy and rely mainly on vegetarian choices. Sweet potatoes are a main part of their menu during these days. Rice pudding is often served as well as black-eyed peas and corn bread. Whole wheat muffins are good, too.

DAY 10
CANDLES

MATERIALS

Snack

PROJECTS

Paraffin Ice Candles: block of paraffin wax (available in the canning section of grocery store), aluminum pie plate, empty ½ pint or 1 pint cardboard carton, string

Dipped Candles: paraffin or colored wax (available in a craft store), candle wicking or string, metal soup can

Beeswax Candles: beeswax, candle wicking or string

Pinecone Candle Holder: corrugated cardboard, glue, paint or ribbon, pinecones and nuts, candle

Candles are a very important part of December holidays. On Christmas trees, they were used for lights before electricity. At Hanukkah, they are part of the nightly celebration in lighting the Menorah. In Kwanzaa, they are also part of the nightly ritual. Adapt these suggestions to fit in appropriately with your situation.

Ask the child why candles are important. They give us light when there is no electricity. They sometimes give off pleasant smells. They are a welcoming sight in a window.

Talk about how candles are made. This part can be done during the craft section.

Candles for Beginners to Make, Alice Gilbreath
Light and Darkness, Franklyn M. Bronley
Rainbow Candles, Myra Shostak
The Night the Lights Went Out, Don Freeman
What Makes a Shadow, Clyde R. Bulla

Paraffin Ice Candles

Melt a block of paraffin wax in a metal pie pan over warm water in a large frying pan. Fill a clean ½ pint or 1 pint milk carton with ice cubes. In the center, wedge a piece of string for the candlewick. When the paraffin is melted, pour over the ice cubes (this is a task for an adult only!) Place the carton in the refrigerator until set. Carefully tear off the carton from around the candle. Your resulting candle will be full of holes.

Beeswax Candles

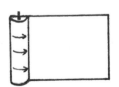

With a pair of scissors cut a sheet of beeswax 3–4" long. Place a length of wick down on one end, letting it stick out about ½". Roll the wax very lightly until the candle is the desired thickness. The finished thickness depends upon the size of your holder.

Dipped Candles

Fill a clean, empty soup can with paraffin or other wax and place in a saucepan filled part way with water. As the wax melts, add more until it is ½" from the top of the can. Dip a piece of string one yard long into the wax. Pull it out and stretch it straight until it hardens. Cut into 6" lengths. Dip one of the pieces into the wax. Remove and let harden, repeat with other pieces. Continue dipping the candles, letting wax harden between each dip. Continue until the candles are the width desired. Cut off the bottoms with a heated knife so that they will stand properly. Roll each candle on a smooth surface to even out the size. Trim wick to ½". (With careful supervision, even fairly young children can do this). It may also be easier to tie a piece of wick to a clothes hanger. The child can dip the candle in by holding onto the top of the hanger, then place the hanger over a doorknob to cool.

Pinecone Candle Holder

Cut two pieces of corrugated cardboard into 4" circles. Cut out a center circle in each the size of the base of the candle you have chosen. Glue the two pieces together. Paint or cover the outside edge with a narrow strip of ribbon. Glue different sized pinecones and nuts onto the top. Place the candle inside, securing with clay.

Candle Fruit Salad

On a small saucer, place a lettuce leaf. Put a pineapple slice on top. Put a small scoop of cottage cheese in the middle. Cut a banana in half and center in the middle of the pineapple slice. Attach a small orange slice or mandarin orange to the top with a toothpick to look like the flame.

DAY 11
GIFTS TO MAKE AND GIVE

MATERIALS
Wrapped gift
Piece of paper, pencil

PROJECTS
Candles: directions in previous chapter

Candle box: cardboard jewelry or other appropriate sized box, white paper, glue or tape, markers or crayons

Pomander: orange, cloves, ribbon, corsage pin

Bookmark: paper, ribbon

Bubble Bath Jar: glass canister, stickers, bubble bath

"Anything" Can: 3 lb. shortening can with plastic lid, spray paint, stickers, pictures, rickrack

Bucket of Goodies: paper paint bucket, appropriate holiday cards, treats to fill

Candy Ring: Styrofoam® ring, straight pins, wrapped candy, candle or ribbon

Wrapping Paper: white shelf paper or wrapping paper, markers, crayons, ink pad, Christmas or Hanukkah cookie cutters

Show the child a wrapped gift (you can put a few pieces of candy, a small toy, or a trinket inside.) Ask him what it is called—it is called a gift or a present. Tell him that in December we give presents to others. Talk about the good feeling that we have inside when we give to others and don't keep thinking about what we are going to receive. You'll want to re-emphasize this again throughout the season.

Ask him to think of the people in the family. Write down the names or draw a picture of each one as he mentions their name. Encourage the child to make a gift for each member of their family.

Talk about other people to whom the child would like to give gifts, such as grandparents and other relatives, neighbors, and teachers. Again, write down a list of the ones to include (encourage them to keep this simple—one or two is fine).

Christmas Books on Gifts
Christmas is a Time for Giving, Joan Walsh Angland
How Santa Claus had a Long and Difficult Journey Delivering His Presents, Fernando Krahn
Melinda's Christmas Stocking, Ruth Jaynes
Something for Christmas, Palmer Brown
The Best Train Set Ever, Pat Hutchins
The Gift, a Portuguese Christmas Tale, Jan B. Balat
The Night It Rained Toys, Dorothy Stephenson

Hanukkah Books on Gifts
Chanukah Surprise, E. and S. Scharfstein

Here are some simple suggestions:

Candles

Choose from any of the candle directions in Day 11 to make as a gift.

Dreidel Present

Make a dreidel as shown in Day 8 as a gift.

Candle Boxes

Make a box for the candles used in Hanukkah and Kwanzaa. Decorate a large jewelry or similar sized box that will hold the 44 candles for Hanukkah or the 7 candles for Kwanzaa. Boxes can also be purchased from stores that do packing and shipping, such as the Mail Boxes, Inc. The box can be covered in white paper. The designs appropriate for each celebration can be drawn on with crayons or markers.

Pomander

Push cloves into an orange until the whole surface is dotted. With a corsage pin, attach a long ribbon to the top so that it can be hung in a closet to freshen the air.

Bookmarks

Have the child color a piece of paper the size of a bookmark. Write "Merry Christmas" and his name and date on the back. A hole can be punched in the top and a ribbon attached.

Another kind of bookmark can be made from felt. Have the child glue on circles, triangles, and other designs of another color to decorate it.

Bubble Bath Jar

Have the child decorate a pretty glass canister with stickers. Fill with bubble bath. Another idea is to just cover the lid with small seashells glued down with a glue gun.

An "Anything Can"

Spray paint an empty, clean can any bright color (perhaps to match the room of the receiver). 3 lb. shortening cans are ideal. Have the child decorate it with stickers, pictures cut from magazines, lace, yarn, or fabric scraps that correspond to the interests of the one who will receive it.

Bucket of Goodies

Glue old Christmas or Hanukkah cards onto the sides of a paper paint bucket. Fill with homemade cookies, candy or other treats.

Candy Ring

Have the child attach pieces of wrapped peppermint or other wrapped candy to a large Styrofoam® ring with small straight pins. Repeat, covering the whole wreath with candy. Put a large candle in the center or attach a ribbon or wire to the back, so that it can be hung.

Wrapping Paper

Children also enjoy decorating their own wrapping paper. Use white shelf or freezer paper. Have the child color it with markers or crayons. Cookie cutters of appropriate shapes for either Hanukkah or Christmas can be traced or stamped with a stamp pad.

In this chapter, the child will learn about the winter season, activities of both animals and people, and enjoy fun in the snow.

DAY 1
WHAT IS WINTER?

MATERIALS
Ice cube
Pictures of winter

PROJECTS
Paper Thermometers: white poster board, red and white ribbon, black marker
Ice Cube Treats: fruit juice, maraschino cherries, banana slices, or pineapple chunks

Talk about what happens in the winter. What does the world look like? (If you live in an area that doesn't have snow or the typical characteristics of winter, talk about how your climate changes.)

Talk about where the leaves have gone, how the grass changed color and the plants died.

Explain that icicles are made of frozen water. Show him one or let him feel an ice cube. Talk about what it feels like, what it tastes like and examine the little bubbles that form inside. If you want, you can melt the icicle or ice cube in a saucepan to further help him understand about icicles.

Take a glass, fill it with water and put it in the freezer. In about an hour (when the outside is frozen and the inside is still liquid), you can see an air bubble, or you can shake the glass and still hear the water. Make a small hole in the top toward one side. Run hot water, over the outside, just until the ice is released from the glass. Drain any water left inside. The resulting "cube" is fun to look at and the child will enjoy eating it.

A Day of Winter, Betty Miles
A Pocketful of Seasons, Doris Foster
All Ready for Winter, Leone Adelson
I Like Winter, Lois Lenski
Stopping by Woods on a Snowy Evening, Robert Frost (with beautiful illustrations by Susan Jeffers)
The Big Snow, Berta and Elmer Hader
The Snowy Day, Ezra J. Keats
Winter is Here, Jane B. Moncure
Winter's Coming, Eve Bunting

Sing a Song of Winter (to the tune of "Sing a Song of Sixpence"—music in Appendix)

Sing a song of winter, frost is in the air.
Sing a song of winter, snowflakes everywhere.
Sing a song of winter, hear the sleigh bells chime.
Can you think of anything as nice as wintertime?

Paper Thermometers

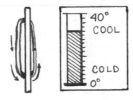

Make thermometers out of paper. Mark degrees between 40 and 0 (or whatever best approximates your temperatures at this time). Or just mark "freezing," "colder," "cold," "chilly," etc., up the side. Cut a slit at the top and bottom. Cut two pieces of ribbon, one red and one white, the length of the thermometer. Glue one end of each together. Insert through slits in paper and glue other ends together on back. The "temperature" can then be made to go up and down as the temperature does outside. (You may want to save this to use in spring when the temperature begins to rise).

Ice Cube Treats

Freeze juice in ice cube trays. Insert a toothpick as a handle. Or put maraschino cherries, banana slices, or pineapple chunks in ice cube trays, cover with water for fruit juice and freeze. Put them in clear soda pop and have as a treat.

Besides the ice treats mentioned above, Popsicles® are also fun for the child.

DAY 2
SNOW AND SNOWFLAKES

MATERIALS
Blue or black construction paper
Magnifying glass

PROJECTS
Snowflakes: white paper, scissors
Dough Snowflakes: salt dough, cookie cutters
Pasta Snowflakes: varied shapes of pasta, glue, gilt spray if desired
String Snowflakes: white string, waxed paper, glue

Talk about how snow is formed. Snow comes from clouds, just as rain does. When it is very cold, the water freezes to form snow crystals which we call snowflakes. If many snow crystals cling together, the snowflakes may be very large.

Talk about snowflakes. All flakes have six sides or six points, but no two are alike, just as fingerprints are all different.

Go outside when it is snowing and allow some flakes to drop onto a dark blue or black piece of construction paper. Quickly look at them with a magnifying glass to observe the different shapes.

Skim a little fresh snow off the ground. Let the child taste it. Place a cup of snow into a saucepan on low heat or at room temperature and let the child see it melt back into water.

Brrr!, James Stevenson
Snow, John Burningham
Snow, Nancy Elizabeth Wallace
Snowtime, Miriam Schlein
The Snowy Day, Ezra J. Keats
White Snow, Bright Snow, Alvin Tresselt

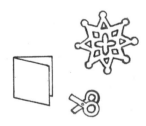

Snowflakes

Cut snowflakes from folded paper. Tape to the windows or hang from a mobile.

String Snowflakes

Form string snowflakes by dipping string in glue and then forming into shapes on waxed paper. These can be hung when dry, too.

Salt Dough Snowflakes

Make salt dough snowflakes, mixing 1 c. salt, 2 c. flour, and 1 c. water. (Add more or less water so the dough is not too sticky). Knead 7-10 minutes. Roll dough about ¼" to ½" thick. Cut into a basic shape with a large cookie cutter or knife. The small details can be cut out with a knife (with Mommy's help) or small hors d'oeuvres cutters. Bake at 325° until golden (about 30 min.). When cool, these can be varnished or spread with glue and sprinkled with glitter. Hang them with yarn or string in a window.

Pasta Snowflakes

Make pasta snowflakes. Lay out different shapes of pasta onto a piece of waxed paper and glue them together to form large snowflakes. Use wagon wheels, corkscrews, bow ties, and other shapes. The finished flakes can be sprayed gold or silver and hung.

Shave or crush ice into glasses. Pour fruit juice or punch over ice and make snow cones.

Make snow cream: fill a bowl with fresh, clean snow and pour maple syrup over and mix. This treat is also good with syrup heated just until boiling and poured over the snow.

DAY 3
WHAT DO ANIMALS DO IN THE WINTER?

MATERIALS
Pictures of animals whose colors
   change in the winter
Snack

PROJECTS
Animal Matching Cards: white poster board, animal patterns or stamps,
   glue, crayons
Winter Cave: card table, blankets

Tell the child that when it's cold, people put on warm clothes. Animals do different things to protect themselves in the winter. Many birds fly south, where the weather is warmer. Some animals hibernate. When the world becomes colder, the animals' bodies tell them to go to sleep. Mammals, such as bears, eat lots of food all summer long and then sleep all winter. Others, such as mice and rabbits, store lots of food in their burrows with them. There, they can eat and stay warm until spring comes.

Show pictures of animals whose colors change in the winter. The fur on rabbits changes from brown to white. The feathers on many birds become duller in color or even white in the winter to blend in with their surroundings.

Angelina's Ice Skates, Katharine Holabird
Bears are Sleeping, Yulya
Buzzy Bear's Winter Party, Dorothy Marino
When Winter Comes, Russell Freedman
Winter Rabbit, Patrick Yee

Animal Matching Cards

Make matching cards for the child to match the animal with where it lives in the winter: butterfly—cocoon; bear—cave; rabbit—hole in the ground; beaver—dam in streams.

Winter Walk

Take a walk in a woods or other natural area. Try to spot the tracks of animals in the snow. Try to decide what animals made the tracks.

Bear Cave

Make a bear "cave" by covering a card table with blankets. This is a fun place to eat lunch, too.

Nuts and raisins or berries mixed together.

Berries (jam) and nuts (peanut butter) can be used for sandwiches.

DAY 4
WHAT DO WE DO IN THE WINTER?

MATERIALS
Pictures of winter clothes
Snack

PROJECTS
Cardboard Mittens: red poster board, red yarn
Snow Scene: baby food jar, plastic figure, moth flakes (remember that these are poisonous), blue food coloring (optional), silicone glue

Show pictures of clothing from magazines or catalogs. Ask which we wear for winter. Why?

Pretend you are going outdoors. Have the child pantomime what he would put on.

Have him pretend that he is skating outside, putting on the skates first. Do the same for skiing, sledding, etc.

Let the child practice zipping his coat and putting on his own boots (depending on his age) to prepare to go outside.

Katy and the Big Snow, Virginia Burton
Snow Fun, Caroline Levine
Snowballs, Lois Ehlert
The Bears' Christmas, Stan and Jan Berenstain (although this story is about a Christmas outing, the bears perform many outdoor winter activities)
The Mitten, Alvin Tresselt

Cardboard Mittens

Cut mittens from red cardboard to hang up. Punch a hole in the bottom of each mitten and string together with red yarn. Write this verse on the mittens:

> "Thumbs in the thumb place,
> Fingers all together,
> This is the song
> We sing in winter weather."

Snowing Paperweight

Thoroughly wash an empty baby food jar, removing the label. Glue a small plastic house, person or animal (available at craft or hobby stores) to inside of lid, let dry. Put 2 T. moth <u>flakes</u> into jar and fill with water, adding a small drop of blue food coloring, if desired. Fill the jar almost to overflowing. Screw on lid to make sure the water level isn't too high. Remove lid; dry it and the jar rim. Glue ridges of lid with silicone glue and screw on tightly. Let it dry for a few hours. The jar can be turned upside down and the snow will fall down on the scene inside. (Remember that moth flakes are poisonous, so be careful when using them around the child.)

Popcorn Snowballs

Make "snowballs" (popcorn balls) to eat.

Snowball Ice Cream Balls

Roll scoops of vanilla ice cream in coconut. Place on a waxed paper covered cookie sheet. Freeze until firm. (These can be served with chocolate syrup if desired).

DAY 5
SNOWMEN

MATERIALS
White paper circles, blue
   construction paper
Snack

PROJECTS
Button Snowman: different sized white buttons, blue construction paper,
   glue, yarn, markers
Cotton Ball Snowman: cotton balls, markers, black felt, twigs or toothpicks
Paper Snowman: white paper, glue, black construction paper, glue, markers

Using cut-out paper circles, build a snowman on blue paper, talking about the different parts. Draw a face, gluing buttons on for eyes, mouth, etc., on the different circles. Take the pieces apart and let the child build the snowman.

Pretend you are building a snowman. Have the child pretend to be the snowman. Ask "What will happen to the snowman?" Have the child pretend to be a melting snowman.

On a cookie sheet or in a sheet cake pan, form three balls out of snow. Add eyes, nose, and other features with raisin or carrot pieces. Watch what happens to the figure when it gets warm inside the house and melts.

Dear Snowman, Janosh
Snowman's Secret, Robert E. Barry
The Self-Made Snowman, Fernando Krahn
The Snowman, Raymond Briggs

The Snowman

A chubby little snowman had a carrot nose
     (form snowman with fist)
Along came a bunny and what do you suppose?
     (hold up two fingers of other hand, hop around)
That hungry little bunny, looking for his lunch
     (rub stomach)
Ate that snowman's carrot nose
     (pretend to bite a carrot)
Crunch, crunch, crunch.
     (pretend to be chewing)

Button Snowmen

Make snowmen from different-sized white buttons glued onto paper. Add yarn for the scarf and draw on a hat.

Cotton Ball Snowman

Glue cotton balls onto colored paper to make snowmen. Make a hat out of black felt. Draw on features with markers. Use twigs or toothpicks for arms.

Snow Picture

Draw a snowman picture. Whip up Ivory Snow soap flakes with a little water until the mixture is the consistency of finger-paint. Let the child draw a picture with it on blue or black construction paper.

Paper Snowman

Make a paper snowman by rolling 2" wide strips of white paper into circles, making three sizes. Add a hat, facial features and arms with black construction paper. Glue on a cardboard base (so it will stand up) or make several, for a mobile.

Marshmallow Snowmen

Make snowmen treats by attaching large marshmallows together with toothpicks, adding miniature chocolate chip features with corn syrup "glue."

Ice Cream Snowmen

Use a large scoop of vanilla ice cream for the body and a marshmallow for the head. Use miniature chocolate chips for the features. A chocolate cookie with a large gumdrop on top can be the hat. These can be made up for the whole family by the child for the evening dessert.

MATERIALS
Snack

PROJECTS
Snow Fort: empty half gallon milk cartons
Snow Castle: bread pans, other metal pans of various sizes
Giant Foot Prints: heavy cardboard, twine or heavy string

This day is spent in outdoor play—parents and kids. If you do not live in an area with snow, you can substitute some of the snowflake projects this day or just skip it. Here are a couple of fun ideas to try:

Snow Fort

Cut the bottoms out of empty half gallon milk cartons. The tops become the "handles." Pack tightly with snow. Remove the "blocks" to make a snow fort. If the snow does not remove easily, the cartons can be sprayed inside with a vegetable spray.

Snow Castle

Make a snow castle. Pack bread pans (or cups, glasses, etc.) with snow. Empty out in various positions to form the turrets, walls, etc., of your castle.

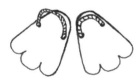

Giant Footprints

Make giant footprints out of heavy cardboard. (you can also make them out of wood if you want them to be more durable and permanent). Center the child's foot on each and make a hole in the cardboard on each side of his foot. Thread heavy string or twine through the holes. Tie the "footprints" onto boots and make monster tracks.

Come inside and drink hot cocoa and eat biscuits or rolls.

Candy Bar Sled

Stick two small candy canes to the sides of a small candy bar with frosting.

DAY 1	CARS
DAY 2	BUSES
DAY 3	TRUCKS
DAY 4	TRAINS
DAY 5	BOATS
DAY 6	AIRPLANES

In this chapter, the child will learn about different forms of transportation, participating in hands-on activities with each.

DAY 1
CARS

MATERIALS
Pictures of cars
Snack

PROJECTS
Cardboard Box Car: large box a child can sit in, butcher paper, markers
Paper Car: white construction paper, crayons, tape

Show pictures of different kinds of cars. Talk about what makes them different. For example, body shapes, number of people they hold, and colors. (Don't feel you have to talk about everything under the hood unless you want to).

Show pictures of old-fashioned cars. Talk about how cars have changed: shape, tires, how they start, features like windshield wipers, lights, etc.

Talk about the different parts of a car—wheels, lights, doors, steering wheel, horn, trunk, engine, window. If you want, you can take him out to the car to show him the parts. This is a good time to explain to him never to play in cars or with the parts of a car.

Talk about how we act around cars:
- Look both ways before crossing streets
- Don't play in the street or ride big wheels or tricycles in the street
- Wear a safety helmet when riding a bike (this is also a good idea for younger ones to start using on their tricycles, etc.)
- Always wear a seat belt or sit in a car seat (for younger children)
- Keep arms and head inside the car
- Keep the doors locked while the car is moving

As a parent, make sure you set a good example and be firm and consistent in expecting the child to obey these safety rules.

ABC of Cars and Trucks, Anne Alexander
Big Yellow Taxi, Ken Wilson-Mas
By Camel or by Car: A Look at Transportation, Guy Billot
Cars and Trucks and Other Vehicles, A First Discovery Book
Cars and Trucks and Things That Go, Richard Scarry
City Poems, Lois Lenski
How Georgina Drove the Car Very Carefully from Boston to New York, Lucy Bate
If I Drove a Car, Miriam Young
Jennifer and Josephine, Bill Peet
Little Old Automobile, Marie Ets
Mr. Frumble's New Cars, Richard Scarry
The Big Book of Things That Go, Caroline Bingham
The Car Book, William Dugan
The Giant Nursery Book of Things That Go, George J. Zaffo
The Great Big Car and Truck Book, Richard Scarry
The Little Auto, Lois Lenski
Wheels, Annie Cobb

Cardboard Box Car

Get a big box the child can sit down in (the size in which cartons of eggs are delivered to the grocery store is perfect). Paint the sides or cover with butcher paper. Decorate so that it will look like a car. Have the child pretend that he is driving around in the car. (Save the box for Day 2, Buses.)

Paper Car

Make a paper car as shown. Have the child color it. Fold and tape.

Candy Bar Race Car

Use a small chocolate covered candy bar. Scoop out a small opening on the top and put an M&M for a steering wheel. Attach round peppermint candies with frosting to make the wheels.

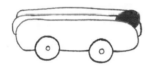

Race Car Hot Dog

See Chapter 7, Day 4, Meat and Fish.

DAY 2
BUSES

MATERIALS
Pictures of buses
Snack

PROJECTS
Bus Picture: yellow construction paper, crayons

Show a picture of a bus. Talk about how it is different from a car (it holds many people, you must pay to ride on it; it travels the same route everyday).

Talk about the different kinds of buses, showing pictures if possible: city bus, school bus, touring bus, double-decker bus.

Talk about the things that a bus driver does: takes the passengers' money, makes sure everyone gets on and off the bus safely, makes sure everyone stays seated (unless the bus is too full—then passengers must stand), checks the engine and lights before leaving so that the bus can travel safely.

Talk about how we ride the bus. Have the child act out waiting for the bus, getting on the bus, paying his fare, quickly finding a seat, staying seated until time to get off, and signaling that he wants to leave.

ABC of Buses, Dorothy Shuttlesworth
Bus Ride, Nancy Jewell
If I Drove a Bus, Miriam Young
The Wheels on the Bus, adapted by Paul O. Zelinsky
General transportation books listed on Day 1

The Bus (song or finger play)
The wheels on the bus go round and round,
Round and round, round and round.
The wheels on the bus go round and round,
All through the town.
    (roll arms around each other to show the wheels going around)
The horn on the bus goes beep, beep, beep,
    (repeat as above pretending to honk a horn)
The wipers on the bus go swish, swish, swish,
    (repeat as above swinging arms back and forth like wiperblades)
The lights on the bus go blink, blink, blink,
    (repeat as above opening and closing hands when you say "blink")

(This can continue with whatever verses you want to add—babies cry "wah, wah, wah," mommies say "shush, shush, shush," money goes "plink, plink, plink," etc.)

146

Box Bus

Using the box from Day 1, remove the old butcher paper. Cover with new paper and have the child decorate it to make the box into a bus as shown.

Bus Picture

Make a bus picture as shown. Have the child draw the people behind the windows.

Bus Ride

Take a ride in a bus. Help the child remember the things that he's practiced.

Cookie Bus

Cut out pieces of rolled dough for the body, wheels, lights, etc. Press smaller pieces onto the body. Bake.

MATERIALS	PROJECTS
Truck pictures	**Milk Carton Truck:** 1 qt. milk carton, construction paper, glue, markers, cardboard, paper fasteners

Show pictures of trucks—talk about all the different kinds of trucks.

Talk about what makes a truck different from a car. The truck is usually heavier. It is used for different kinds of jobs rather than just carrying people. It generally has bigger tires to go over rougher ground and to carry heavier loads, etc.

Help the child learn to identify several frequently seen trucks: delivery truck, dump truck, pick-up truck, garbage truck, cement mixer, semi-trailer.

If I Drove A Truck, Miriam Young
Let's Go Trucks, David L. Harrison (A Little Golden Book)
Machines at Work, Byron Barton
Mike Mulligan and His Steam Shovel, Virginia Burton
Road Builders, B.G. Hennessy
The Big Book of Real Trucks, George J. Zaffo
The Truck of the Track, Janet Burroway
Truck Drivers: What Do They Do?, Carla Greene
General transportation books listed in Day 1

Milk Carton Truck

From an empty one-quart milk carton, make a semi-trailer. Cover the carton with paper. Draw on features. Cut wheels from cardboard and attach them with paper fasteners. These can also be made from different-sized cartons to make other kinds of trucks.

Construction Site Field Trip

Visit a construction site. Let the child watch the trucks and talk about the job that each truck does.

Since some trucks carry food, during your snack time talk about how the food was brought by a truck from the manufacturer or farmer to your supermarket.

DAY 4
TRAINS

MATERIALS
Train pictures
Snack

PROJECTS
Box Train: small boxes, construction paper, markers, yarn, glue

Show a picture of an old train. Talk about the parts—smokestack, wheels, bell, light, engineer's seat, wood or coal bin, engine.

Show a picture of a modern train. Talk about the new parts—whistle instead of bell, more wheels, diesel engines that burn fuel oil like cars instead of coal or wood. Explain that modern trains travel much more quickly than the old ones.

Show pictures of the different cars on a train. On a freight train, these could include the coal car, cattle car, flat car, oil car, caboose. On a passenger train, these could include pullman, dining car, coach car and scenic domeliner. Help the child learn the names. (If you have problems identifying these, most train books listed below will be helpful in explaining the parts of a train and what the parts are for).

Freight Train, Donald Crews
Hop Aboard! Here We Go!, Richard Scarry
If I Drove A Train, Miriam Young
Little Red Caboose, Miriam Potter (A Little Golden Book)
The Big Book of Real Trains, Elizabeth Cameron
The Caboose Who Got Loose, Bill Peet
The Everyday Train, Amy Ehrlich
The Little Engine That Could, Watty Piper
The Little Train, Graham Greene
The Little Train, Lois Lensky
Two Little Trains, Margaret Brown
General transportation books listed in Day 1

I've Been Working on the Railroad

I've been working on the railroad, all the live long day.
I've been working on the railroad, just to pass the time away.
Can't you hear the whistle blowing? Rise up so early in the morn?
Can't you hear the captain shouting, Dinah, blow your horn?
Dinah, won't you blow? Dinah, won't you blow?
Dinah, won't you blow your horn?
Dinah, won't you blow? Dinah, won't you blow?
Dinah, won't you blow your horn?
Someone's in the kitchen with Dinah.
Someone's in the kitchen I know.
Someone's in the kitchen with Dinah
Strumming on the old banjo and singing
Fee, fi, fiddly-i-o. Fee, fi, fiddly-i-o-o-o.
Fee, fi, fiddly-i-o. Strumming on the old banjo.

Chair Train

Make a "train" from chairs. Let the child pretend to be different workers on a train—engineer, conductor, porter.

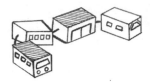

Box Train

Make a box train using small boxes, such as those for jewelry, perfume, and tissue. Cover the boxes with paper decorated as different train cars, then attach together by punching holes in the ends of the boxes, threading pieces of yarn through, and knotting the ends.

Pretend to be eating in the dining car during snack time.

DAY 5
BOATS

MATERIALS
Boat pictures
Boat Eggs: eggs, cheese, toothpick

PROJECTS
Paper Boats: paper
Plastic Boats: plastic containers (margarine, etc.), string

Show pictures of different kinds of boats. Talk about the sizes and shapes. Help him understand that a ship is a big boat.

Talk about the many ways that boats are powered: muscle power—canoes, kayaks, row boats; wind—sailboats, schooners; motors—speedboats, ships, ocean liners; fuel and paddle—paddle wheelers.

Have him pretend he is on a boat. He can rock gently back and forth. He can pretend to see seagulls and fish, perhaps even pretend to fish.

Burt Dow, Deep-Water Man, Robert McCloskey
Great Steamboat Mystery, Richard Scarry
Henry the Castaway, Mark Taylor
If I Sailed a Boat, Miriam Young
Little Toot series, Hardie Gramatky
The Big Book of Real Boats and Ships, George J. Zaffo
The Boats on the River, Marjorie Flack
The Little Sailboat, Lois Lenski
Tim series, Edward Ardizzone

Row, Row, Row Your Boat

Row, row, row your boat,
Gently down the stream.
Merrily, merrily, merrily, merrily,
Life is but a dream.

Plastic Boats

Make boats from empty plastic containers such as margarine or non-dairy whipping cream. Punch holes on the sides at the top edge, and tie together to make a whole fleet for your bathtub.

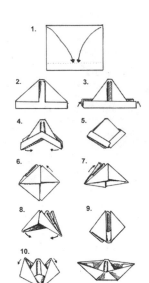

Paper Boats

Make paper boats, as shown.
1. Fold a piece of construction paper in half.
2. Fold corners down to an inch from the bottom.
3. Fold bottom edges up.
4. Bring outside edges together.
5. Flatten.
6. Bring one bottom point up to top and crease.
7. Bring other bottom point up and crease.
8. Bring ends together again.
9. Flatten.
10. Pull sides back out.

Float the boats in the bathtub or a nearby stream.

Boat Eggs

Cut peeled hard-boiled eggs in half. Mash yolks and add mayonaise as desired. Stuff back in white halves. Make a sail from a slice of cheese threaded with a toothpick.

DAY 6
AIRPLANES

MATERIALS
Airplane pictures

PROJECTS
Paper Airplanes: white paper, crayons
Tongue Depressor Helicopters: tongue depressor, thumb tack or small nail, pencil with eraser or small dowel
Paper Helicopter: white construction paper, glue or tape

Show pictures of different kinds of airplanes. Let him see old-fashioned planes as well as modern jets.

Talk about the parts of a plane—wings, cockpit (where the pilot sits), tail, propellers, or jet engines.

Talk about helicopters and how they are different from airplanes: propellers on top; can go up and down rather than taking off on a runway. (Again, if you have problems identifying these, check in the books listed below.)

Angela's Airplane, Robert N. Munsch
Fly High, A Little Golden Book
If I Flew A Plane, Miriam Young
Little Red Plane, Ken Wilson-Max
Loopy, Hardie Gramatky
Richard Scarry's Great Big Air Book, Richard Scarry
The Big Book of Real Airplanes, George J. Zaffo
The Little Airplane, Lois Lenski
We Fly, Alfred Olscheski
General transportation books listed on Day 1

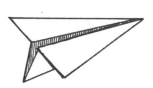

Paper Airplanes

Make paper airplanes to fly. Have the child decorate them with crayons. Here's an example if you, like me, never made a paper airplane until you became a parent.

Tongue Depressor Helicopters

Make tongue depressor helicopters. Put a thumb tack or small nail through the center of a tongue depressor. Attach to the eraser end of a pencil or to the top of a small dowel. Hold the stick vertically and rub between the palms of your hands with the depressor on top. Let go and the "helicopter" will take off.

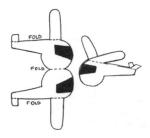

Paper Helicopter

Make a paper helicopter. Draw the helicopter outline on a heavy piece of paper, folding as shown on the dotted lines. Glue or tape the two sides of the helicopter together. This is fun to hold up high, or stand at the top of the stairs and let it twirl down.

Lifesaver Airplanes

Use two rolls of lifesavers, one stick of gum, one rubber band. Put together as shown.

DAY 1	MAIL CARRIERS
DAY 2	LETTERS
DAY 3	FIREFIGHTERS
DAY 4	POLICE OFFICERS
DAY 5	GARBAGE COLLECTORS & RECYCLING
DAY 6	OTHER WORKERS

In this chapter, the child will learn about workers in the community who help us and protect us. He should be able to identify police officers, mail carriers, firefighters, and others. He will also begin to have an understanding of the importance of recycling and learn to recycle.

DAY 1
MAIL CARRIERS

MATERIALS
Letters
Snack

PROJECTS
Mail Carrier Hats: lunch bags, marker
Mail Bags: grocery bags, string, crayons, or stickers

Show some letters and ask how they got to your home.

Watch for your mail carrier and have the child say "hi" to him or her. The child can then ask him/her what a mail carrier does on the job.

Talk about the equipment mail carriers need to deliver the mail: trucks to get around in, bags to carry all the letters, mailboxes to put the mail into, etc.

Walk down the block and look at all the different mailboxes. Have the child notice that the houses have numbers on them, so the mail carrier knows where to deliver the mail. (If you live in an apartment building, adapt this for your situation).

Act out being a mail carrier: sorting the letters into different boxes at the post office, placing them in the mailbag, walking down the street to deliver them.

(Note: Mail the child a letter he can receive on Day 2)

Country Mailman, Jerrold Beim
First Class!, Harold Roth
The Post Office Book, Gail Gibbons (excellent)

Mail Carrier Hats

Make mail carrier hats. Cut lunch bags down to a 5" height with the front cut in a semicircle for the brim as shown. Write "U.S. Mail" on the front of the hat.

Mailbags

Make little mailbags out of large grocery bags. Tie string through the top to fit over the child's shoulder. The child can color his bag or place stickers on it to resemble stamps.

DAY 2
LETTERS

MATERIALS
Letters
White paper, marker
Snack

PROJECTS
Mailing Letters: stationary, envelopes, stamps

Show several letters to the child. Ask him how the mail carrier knew that they belonged to your family. Point out the address. Give him the letter you wrote on Day 1 that the mail carrier delivered to your home. Read it to him.

On a large piece of paper, draw a pretend envelope. Talk about the return address (where the letter is from), the address (where the letter is to go), and the stamp (to pay for it to get there).

Let the child write a letter to someone special: a relative or friend. Have him lick the stamp for the envelope (Be sure to emphasize that stamps are only for licking with your permission or you may find all your stamps carefully stuck to the wall, as I once did!)

Let him write letters with your assistance or draw pictures to other family members. Give him fake stamps (stickers, Christmas seals, etc.) to put on them. Have the child put them in his mailbag and deliver one to the dresser or room of each member of the family.

A Letter to Amy, Ezra Keats
Adventures of a Letter, G. William Schloat
At the Post Office, Carol Greene
Linda's Air Mail Letter, Norman Bell
On Beyond Zebra, Theodor Seuss Geisel

Mailing Letters

Take the letters he's written to a relative or friend and mail them at the post office. You may be able to arrange a short tour, so the child can see what will happen to his letter.

DAY 3
FIREFIGHTERS

MATERIALS
Pictures of firefighters
Raincoats and boots (optional)
Snack

PROJECTS
Fire Hats: red 18" x 12" construction paper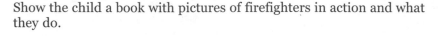

Show the child a book with pictures of firefighters in action and what they do.

Show a toy fire truck. Talk about the different parts, such as the ladder, hose, and siren. Ask what he thinks they are used for.

Show pictures of what firefighters wear. Have the child pretend he is putting on the heavy pants, boots, coat, and hat.

Visit a fire hydrant in your neighborhood. Talk about what it is called and how the firefighters use it.

Use this time to talk to the child about the dangers of fire and matches. Help him fully understand that matches are for adults, not children. Tell him not to stand too close to a fire in the fireplace because little sparks could fly out and burn him. Also, if you have a kerosene heater in the winter time, make sure he understands that it can burn him. Fire stations frequently have illustrated booklets to teach children about fire and safety, too.

Big Book of Real Fire Engines, George J. Zaffo
Blue Bug's Safety Book, Virginia Poulet
Fire Truck, A Mighty Machines Book
Fireman Brown, Harry Bernstein
Fireman Save My Cat!, Tony Palazzo
Fireman Small, Lois Lenski
Fireman Small, Wong Herbert Lee
I Want to be a Fireman, Graham Greene
Jim Fireman, Roger Bester
The Big Book of Fire Engines, Elizabeth Cameron
The Bravest Fireman, Leah Zytman
The Busiest Firefighters Ever, Richard Scarry (a VHS tape)
The Little Fire Engine, Lois Lenski

Fire Engine Song (song in Appendix)

Down the street the engine goes
The firemen chase the fire
Up the ladder with their hose
Out goes the fire.

Fire Hats

From red construction paper, cut out a fire hat, following the directions in Chapter 10, Day 3, Pilgrims and Thanksgiving, for Pilgrim hats. However, rather than cutting the brim in a circle, extend the back end 4 ½" as shown.

Wearing his red hat, raincoat, and boots, the child can play fire fighter. Perhaps you have an old small piece of hose he can also use.

A Visit to the Fire Station

This is a great day to visit the fire station. Call ahead a week or two in advance. I have found the firefighters to be more than helpful, even if you are just taking one or two children on a tour.

DAY 4
POLICE OFFICERS

MATERIALS
Pictures of police officers
Snack

PROJECTS

Talk about the many things police officers do: help people drive their cars safely, help children cross the street, help children get home when they are lost (emphasize the good!)

Have the child pretend he is lost, and you are the police officer. Ask him questions such as: "What is your name?"; "What is your Daddy's name?"; "Where do you live?"; and "What is your phone number?" (Although he may be a little young for this, he needs to learn this information as early as possible).

Try to get a book from the library with pictures of what the police do (see bibliography below). Don't read the words to the child as much as talk to him about what is going on in the pictures.

This is an important time for the child to learn that the police are his friends. Don't use police officers as "meanies," who are going to come and put him in jail when he is naughty. Police help and protect us, and children will do so much better in their relationships with police officers if this is emphasized.

Green Says, "Go", Ed Emberly
I Want to be a Police Officer, Donna Baker
Make Way for Ducklings, Robert McCloskey (a family of ducks is befriended by a kind policeman)
My Daddy is a Policeman, Elizabeth Ann Doll
Officer Buckle & Gloria, Peggy Rathmann
On the Beat—Policeman at Work, Barry Robinson and Martin Dain
Policeman Small, Lois Lenski
Red Light, Green Light, Margaret Wise Brown
Safety Can Be Fun, Munro Leaf
Sergeant Murphy's Day Off, a Richard Scarry VHS tape
Signs, Ron and Nancy Goor

Twinkle, Twinkle Traffic Light (sung to the tune of "Twinkle, Twinkle Little Star," fun to act out, too)

Twinkle, twinkle traffic light,
Shining on the corner bright.
When it's green, it's time to go.
When it's red, it's stop you know.
Twinkle, twinkle traffic light.
Shining on the corner bright.

Visit to the Police Station

Make arrangements a week or two in advance and visit a police station today. Our oldest son had a marvelous time at age four on this visit. One police officer even let him push his car siren for a few seconds.

Safety Walk

Take a walk though your neighborhood or on a downtown street, following the signs and looking both directions when you cross the streets. Point out that some signs are for cars (speed limit, STOP sign, YIELD sign, etc.) some are for people (crosswalk lines, WALK/DON'T WALK sign, "sidewalk closed," etc.), and others are for both (traffic lights).

DAY 5
GARBAGE COLLECTORS AND RECYCLING

MATERIALS

Recyclable items: glass bottle, newspaper, metal cans, soft drink cans, plastic milk jugs, plastic grocery bags, vegetable peelings, coffee grounds, etc.
Examples of recycled paper, pencils, etc.
Snack

PROJECTS

Celery Pollution: piece of celery, glass of water, food coloring
Litter Walk: garbage bags

Talk about what we do with the things we don't want—we throw them away. But there are different ways to "throw things away." Some things can be used again in a different way, and we call this "recycling."

Show food items we can recycle, such as egg shells, vegetable peelings, etc. If you have a garden, put these in a plastic bag during the coming weeks and then add them to your compost pile (see activity below).

Explain that certain items can be used again. If your community provides curbside recycling, show the child how you divide these items for the garbage collectors. Allow your child to place these items in the appropriate spot in the coming weeks, so he can help with this.

If you have examples of recycled items, show them to the child and explain what happened so they can be used again.

50 Simple Things Kids Can Do to Save the Earth, The EarthWorks Group
101 Ways to Save Money and Save Our Planet, The Green Group
Earth Dance, Joanne Ryder
Going Green: A Kid's Handbook to Saving the Planet, J. Elkington, J. Hailes, D. Hill and J. Makower

Celery Pollution

Fill a clear glass with water and add food coloring or ink, so that the water becomes dark. Explain that this is like the water in our rivers or lakes which has become polluted by bad chemicals. Cut off the bottom of a stalk of celery and place in the glass. In a few hours, the celery will have absorbed the dark color and will look awful.

162

Litter Walk

Pretend to be garbage collectors for the world around you. Carrying plastic garbage bags, take a walk through your neighborhood or a nearby park, and pick up the trash that has been thrown on the ground. Because of the danger of a child cutting himself on a broken bottle or open can, have him just pick up the paper and you pick up the other items. This will be even more effective if you can carry two bags and put the recyclable items in one and the nonrecyclables in the other.

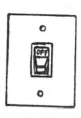

Other Things You Can Do

Use cloth grocery bags, turn off lights when you leave the room, turn in your Christmas tree at designated pickup stations, use both sides of paper (especially for the activities in this book), cut the plastic rings from 6-packs of drinks, re-use aluminum foil, use cloth towels instead of paper.

DAY 6
OTHER WORKERS IN YOUR COMMUNITY

MATERIALS
Snack

PROJECTS
Pellon™ City: Pellon™ interfacing purchased from a fabric store, markers, little cars

Have the child think of other people who help us. Ask: "When Daddy's suits or Mommy's sweaters are dirty, where do we take them?" (cleaners), "When we need some food, where do we go? (grocery store). Continue on with barber, butcher, hardware store clerk, druggist, gas station attendant, etc.

Have him pretend that he is going into a store and needs some help. Help him learn to speak to other people with confidence. Have him practice asking questions such as: "Where do you keep your dolls?"; "Where's the ice cream?"; "How much are the cookies?"; etc. You can stand behind a counter or a table, and the child can ask you for help.

City Poems, Lois Lenski
City Workers, JeanneRowe
Road Builders, B.G. Hennessy
Sara's City, Sue Alexander
There Is a Town, Gail Herman
Wake Up City, Alvin Tresselt

Pellon™ City

On a large piece of Pellon™ interfacing, draw a city with markers. Include buildings for the different helpers you've talked about this week, homes, stop signs on the corners, etc. The child can then drive little cars or walk with fingers through the town and visit the helpers.

Field Trip to Visit a Helper

You might want to take the child on a field trip to visit a drugstore, a barbershop, or a gas station. Ask the owner to explain to the child what he or she does.

Thaw a loaf of frozen bread dough (or make your own if you wish), and have the child pretend he is a baker in a bakery. He can form the bread into tiny loaves or rolls. Let rise 30 minutes. Brush with melted butter and bake at 375° until done (around 25 min.).

DAY 1	TAKING CARE OF OUR BODIES
DAY 2	DENTISTS AND TEETH
DAY 3	DOCTORS

In this chapter, the child will learn about the importance of keeping clean, brushing his teeth and hair, and getting enough sleep. He will learn a little about germs and how to protect himself and others from getting sick. He will also learn about dentists and doctors and the roles that they play in keeping us well.

DAY 1
TAKING CARE OF OUR BODIES

MATERIALS
Bar of Soap
Facial tissue, rubber band
Snack

PROJECTS
Soap Bubbles: glycerin (available from a drug store), dishwashing liquid, straw or small funnel
Soap Painting: Ivory Snow® or any soap flakes, freezer paper or white shelf paper
Personal Hygiene Items: small package of facial tissue, soap, and hand lotion

Talk about the importance of taking baths, washing hair, and changing into clean underwear and clothes each day. Let him brush your hair and talk about how brushing hair will not only keep it looking nice, but will also make it shiny.

Show a bar of soap and ask what it's used for. Ask, "How does it smell?" (You might want to have several kinds to smell). Place it in some water and rub your hands back and forth to make bubbles. Talk about how the bubbles carry the dirt and germs away. Explain that germs are little bugs that we can't see but can make us sick. Show the child how to wash his hands properly. Let him try it in either a dishpan or a sink.

Make a puppet for your hand by putting a facial tissue over your fist and securing it with a rubber band around your wrist. A face can then be drawn on the tissue with marker by you or the child. (If you draw it on, make sure that you've put the puppet on the opposite hand from the one you write with!) Let this puppet talk about how we take care of sneezes and runny noses, using a tissue to catch the germs.

Talk about how important it is for our bodies to eat good food and get enough sleep. Tell them a story about a little car and how it ran out of gas because it had been driven too long. Then it overheated because it hadn't had a rest. Our bodies need "fuel" and rest to help them keep going.

Depending upon the age of your child, you can talk to them about vitamins and minerals. Explain that these are special helpers that make us strong and healthy. They are found in good food. We need certain amounts of them in order to stay well and grow up big and tall.

Finally, discuss the importance of exercise. When we use our muscles, they become strong and we feel better. Open and close your hand several times. Explain that the muscles are what makes this happen.

Andrew's Bath, David McPhail
Casey in the Bath, Cynthis DeFelice
There Is a Town, Gail Herman
Kiss the BooBoo, Sue Tarsky
Minnie the Mump, Paul Tripp
Phoebe Dexter has Harriet Peterson's Sniffles, Laura Numeroff
The Bubble Factory, Tomie de Paola

166

Soap Bubbles

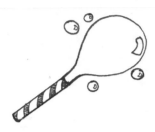

Buy or make soap bubbles that the child can blow with either a straw or a small funnel (dip the large end into a bubble mixture and blow out the small end). You can also use juice cans with the ends removed, coat hangers in interesting shapes, Slinkys®, or any sized hoops. Here is a good recipe for homemade bubbles:

> 2 c. warm water
> 6 T. glycerin (available at drug store)
> 6 T. Dawn® dishwashing liquid
> dash sugar

Mix well. Let stand in an open container at least one day before using.

Soap Painting

Make finger-paint by mixing Ivory Snow® (or any soap flakes) with enough water to make a thick paste. Whip until it's the consistency of heavy cream. Separate portions into paper cups and add different food colorings. Paint on the shiny side of freezer paper (it's less expensive than finger-paint paper) or let the child paint the inside of the bathtub. When he is through, just turn on the water and give him a bubble bath!

Personal Hygiene Items

Give your child his own package of facial tissue, soap and hand lotion (you can often buy samples at the drug store which are good for this).

DAY 2
DENTISTS AND TEETH

MATERIALS
White paper tooth, brown paper "spots," large brush (such as a car snow brush)
Toothbrush and toothpaste
Disclosing tablets

PROJECTS
Play Dough Teeth: play dough (recipe in Appendix)

Ask the child who helps him keep his teeth clean. Then have him describe what a dentist does. If you have a young child who has not yet seen the dentist, take the time to explain more.

Pretend you are a dentist and look at their teeth. Count how many teeth they have and tell them how nice and white they look.

Put a large drawing of a tooth on the board or wall. Put brown spots of paper on it to show food and sugar. Use a large brush to remove them—I use the snow brush from the car. Tape the brown spots on very lightly, so they can easily be removed by the brush.

Have the child brush his teeth. Then have him chew red disclosing tablets (available from your dentist or drug store). Let the child see the places where he needs to brush better—where his teeth have red left on them from the tablets. Then have him brush again, paying particular attention to those areas.

Many dentists recommend that parents brush their children's teeth until the kids are in school. Sometimes the child objects, so this example of the red disclosing tablets helps him see why he needs a parent's help. While I brush my child's teeth, however, I explain to them what I am doing—brushing all the surfaces. When I floss their teeth (which should be done once a day), I also explain what I'm doing and why.

A Visit to the Dentist, Garn
A Visit to the Dentist, Mary Packard
Albert's Toothache, Barbara Williams
Alligator's Toothache, Diane de Groat
Barney Goes to the Dentist, Linda Dowdy
Brush Your Teeth Please, Leslie McGuire and Jean Pidgeon (a great pop-up book)
How Many Teeth?, Paul Showers
Little Bear Brushes His Teeth, Jutta Langrenter
Little Rabbit's Loose Tooth, Lucy Bates
My Dentist, Anne Rockwell
My Dentist, My Friend, P.K. Halliman
My Little Friend Goes to the Dentist, Evelyn M. Finnegan
The Mango Tooth, Charlotte Pomerantz
The Missing Tooth, Joanna Cole

I Have a Little Toothbrush

I have a little toothbrush,	(pretend to hold a toothbrush)
I hold it very tight.	(pretend to hold tightly)
I brush my teeth each morning	(pretend to brush)
And then again at night.	(repeat brushing)
So when I see the dentist,	
He tells me I'm all right.	(smile)
My teeth are bright and shiny,	(point to teeth)
Now what do you think of that?	
Brush, brush, brush, brush,	
Brush, brush, splat!	(pretend to brush then spit)

Play Dough Teeth

Make teeth and a toothbrush out of play dough. Have the child put darker pieces of play dough on the teeth where food might hide. Show them how brushing can eliminate these.

Personal Brush and Toothpaste

Give your child a new toothbrush and a small tube of toothpaste.

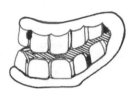

Serve a treat such as yogurt, cheese or ice cream made with a milk product. Explain that milk is very good for our teeth because it contains calcium which helps make teeth and bones strong.

MATERIALS
Picture of doctor
Snack

PROJECTS
Doctor's Kit: egg carton, yarn, empty spool of thread, tongue depressor or Popsicle® stick, cardboard, aluminum foil, candy stick

Ask who helps us get better when we are sick. Talk about the doctor and about what a nice person he or she is.

Bring a play doctor's kit and talk about what the different instruments are used for—stethoscope, thermometer, otoscope (to look in ears), tongue depressor, reflex hammer.

Talk about the reasons we visit the doctor's office. Help him feel comfortable with the experiences that he has had. Help him understand that although doctors have to sometimes hurt us (when they give shots, for example), they care about us and want us to feel well and happy.

A Visit to the Hospital, Dan Elliott
A Visit to the Hospital, Francine Chase
Arthur's Eyes, Marc Brown
Betsy and the Doctor, Gunilla Wolde
Cromwell's Glasses, H. Keller
Curious George Goes to the Hospital, H.R. Rey
Doctors and Nurses, Graham Greene
Jeff's Hospital Book, Harriet Sobol
Madeline, Ludwig Bemelmans
Muffy in the Hospital, Dick Bruna
Nicky Goes to the Doctor, Richard Scarry
Going to the Doctor, Fred Rogers

Five Little Monkeys

Five little monkeys jumping on the bed.
    (five fingers from one hand "jump" on the other palm)
One fell off and bumped his head.
    (hold head in hands)
Momma called the doctor
    (pretend to dial and hold receiver)
And the doctor said,
"There'll be no more monkeys, jumping on the bed!
    (shake finger in mock anger)

(Repeat eliminating a monkey each time on down to "No little monkeys jumping on the bed").

Miss Polly's Dolly

Miss Polly had a dolly, who was sick, sick, sick.
    (with a sad smile, pretend to rock doll)
So, she called for the doctor to come quick, quick, quick!
    (pretend to dial the telephone)
The doctor came with his bag and his hat.
    (pretend to put on a hat and carry bag)
And he knocked on the door with rat-a-tat-tat.
    (pretend to knock on door)
He looked at the dolly and he shook his head.
    (shake head)
He said, "Miss Polly, put her straight to bed."
    (shake finger)
He wrote on the paper for a pill, pill, pill.
    (pretend to write on paper)
"I'll be back in the morning with my bill, bill, bill."
    (wave good-bye)

Doctor Kits

Help the child make his own doctor kit and then he can pretend with dolls that he is a doctor:

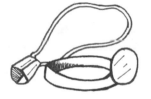

Stethoscope: one compartment from an egg carton strung with yarn or string

Otoscope: empty spool of thread glued to a tongue depressor

Mirror: circle of cardboard covered with foil and stapled to a paper headband

Thermometer: a candy stick

Tongue depressor

Serve any apple treat, such as sliced apples or an apple turnover, and tell the child the old saying: "An apple a day keeps the doctor away." (You might want to mention that this is only a saying, and an orange a day is just as good.)

DAY 1	WHAT IS VALENTINE'S DAY?
DAY 2	MAKING VALENTINES
DAY 3	LET'S HAVE A VALENTINE PARTY

In this chapter, the child will learn about Valentine's Day and the symbols that surround it. He will participate in several activities involving hearts and the making of valentines for family and friends, culminating in a Valentine's Party.

DAY 1
WHAT IS VALENTINE'S DAY?

MATERIALS
Red paper heart
White doily
Picture of Cupid
Snack

PROJECTS
Chalk Drawing Hearts: red construction paper hearts, white chalk
Heart Necklace: red construction paper hearts, yarn, needle, soda straws
Fabric Hearts: red material or felt, white yarn, needle
Heart Tree: dead tree branch, red construction paper, red yarn, jar or can, small pebbles or marbles

Hold up a red paper heart. Ask what is it. (a heart) Now put a doily behind it. Now what is it? (a valentine)

Talk about Valentine's Day as one special day during the year when we let people we love know how much we care for and appreciate them. (There are several stories about how Valentine's Day was started, but I don't think they add to the chapter for this age group, so I didn't cover them).

Show a picture of cupid. Explain that we sometimes see this boy's picture around Valentine's Day. His name is Cupid. He supposedly shoots magic arrows at people to make them love each other. He helps us to remember to make other people happy. Ask how we can make others happy.

A Village Full of Valentines, James Stevenson
Miss Flora McFlimsey's Valentine, Mariana
Our Valentine Book, Jane Moncure
Valentine's Day, Joyce Kessel

Chalk Drawing Hearts

Color with white chalk on red construction paper hearts.

Heart Necklace

Let the child string small precut paper hearts on yarn with a needle. Separate each heart with 1" pieces of soda straw. The garland can be made into a necklace or used to decorate the room.

Fabric Hearts

Again with white yarn and a large needle, let the child sew back and forth through red material or felt hearts to make a design.

Heart Tree

Make a heart tree. Cut out various sizes of hearts from red paper. Tape or tie a piece of string to each heart. Tie the hearts to a small, dead tree branch. Support the branch in a jar or a can filled with small pebbles or marbles.

Candy or conversation hearts

Small box of chocolates

MATERIALS

Valentines: homemade or
  purchased
Snack

PROJECTS

Valentine Animals: different sizes of construction paper hearts, glue, marker
  or crayon

Again talk about why we send valentines. Have the child think of someone special to give a valentine. Perhaps he will think of a lonely
neighbor, a grandparent, or a special person he knows such as a teacher
at church, the mailman or a friend. (Remember that small children are
usually very happy to only give one or two valentines.)

Arthur's Big Valentine, Lilliam Hoban
Bee My Valentine!, Miriam Cohen
Little Love Story, Fernando Krahn
Pleasant Fieldmouse's Valentine Trick, Jan Wahl
She Loves Me, She Loves Me Not, Robert Keeshan

Sending Valentines

Sign and address either homemade or store valentines for the friends
and family discussed above. Help the child take the valentines to them.

Valentine Animals

Glue together different sizes of construction paper hearts. Add extra
details such as eyes, legs, etc., with a marker or crayon.

Make and frost valentine cookies for the family.

DAY 3
LET'S HAVE A VALENTINE PARTY

MATERIALS

PROJECTS
Heart Relay Race: red construction paper hearts; marker
Party Refreshments: pretzels, frosting, red flavored Jell-O®, cupcakes

Children enjoy simple games at their parties. You may want to invite several of your child's friends to participate with him this day.

Heart Relay Race

Cut out hearts from red construction paper. With a marker, write on each of them an action your child has mastered such as crawl, somersault, hop, skip, jump, walk backwards. If you have enough children, make teams. Call out one of the activities, and they can race. With just one or two children, have them pick a heart; you read them their word, and have them do it down to the end of the room and back. They also think it's fun if Mommy does this, too!

Find the Hearts

Hide tiny hearts around the room and let them try to find them.

What Am I Thinking Of?

Have them take turns thinking of as many things as they can that are red.

Make cupcakes and frost with pink or red frosting.

Serve any flavor red Jell-O® (strawberry, cherry, etc.).

Frosted pretzels (they look like little hearts)

> 1 can vanilla frosting with red food coloring added, or your
> favorite frosting
> 1 package pretzels

Melt frosting in top of double boiler until liquid. Remove from heat but leave frosting over hot water. Dip pretzels into frosting, then place on waxed paper. Let dry 8 hrs. This could be a fun activity to make and eat for the party. Then extras can be served to the rest of the family for dessert.

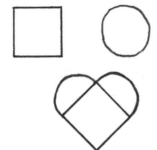

Heart Shaped Cake

Following directions in a package of cake mix, bake a 9"-round and a 9"-square cake. Place square cake on plate. Cut round cake in half as shown. Frost.

Giant Kisses

Follow recipe for Marshmallow Treat Nests (recipe in Appendix) using Rice Krispies® or chocolate rice cereal. Put mixture into a large buttered funnel. Let cool, unmold and wrap in plastic wrap.

DAY 1	WHAT IS THE OCEAN?
DAY 2	FISH
DAY 3	SHELLS AND SHELLFISH

The child will have the opportunity to learn about the world within the ocean. He will learn about fish and shellfish with activities to increase his understanding of colors through sorting and matching and improve his small motor skills as he creates a mosaic fish picture.

DAY 1
WHAT IS THE OCEAN?

MATERIALS

Pictures of the ocean and
    things in it
Sand
Snack

PROJECTS

Brick Coral: brick or coal, small aluminum pie plate or saucer, non-iodized
    salt, liquid laundry bluing, household ammonia

Show pictures of the ocean. Talk about how the water comes in and out
in waves. Sometimes the water goes up high on the beach and sometimes it is low—we call these tides. The tides come in and out every day.

Talk about sand. It is found on the shores of nearly all oceans and is
formed when rocks are broken up into tiny bits. If you look at ocean
sand closely, you can see bits of shells broken up on the shore.

Talk about how the water in the ocean has salt in it. Let the child have a
sip of water to which you've added ½ tsp. of salt. Ask him how it tastes.
Explain that the animals and plants that live in the ocean need to have
salt in their water to live.

Talk about what we find in the oceans: fish, shell fish, coral, seaweed,
octopus and squid families. If possible, show pictures of these.

A Day at the Beach, Mircea Vasiliu
Blue Bug's Beach Party, Virginia Poulet
Harry by the Sea, Gene Zion
The Bears' Nature Guide, Stan and Jan Berenstain, pg. 38-39
Under the Ocean, Eugene Booth (a great thinking book)
When the Tide is Low, Sheila Cole

Brick Coral

Grow your own "coral." Place several pieces of broken brick or soft coal
the size of large walnuts in a small 6" aluminum pie pan or saucer.
Then mix together:

4 T. non-iodized salt
4 T. liquid bluing (available in laundry section of the supermarket)
4 T. water
1 T. household ammonia

Slowly pour mixture over pieces in dish. Then carefully drop small
amounts of food coloring over the bricks. In just a short time, little
crystals will begin to form. Don't move the pan around too much or
touch the "coral," because it will crumble easily.

Visit to the Ocean

If you live near the ocean, plan a visit for the day and let the child see many of the things you have talked about.

Make or buy salt water taffy as a treat this day.

Serve goldfish crackers (let child pretend he's a big fish eating little fish).

MATERIALS
Pictures of fish
Snack

PROJECTS
Fishing Game: cardboard or poster board, paint or crayons, magnetic strips, paper clips, string, dowel or stick

Mosaic Fish Picture: heavy cardboard, marker, fillers such as popcorn, beans, rice, etc.

Show pictures of fish. Talk about the different parts of the fish and what they are used for. The tail helps the fish move through the water. Fins help the fish change directions. Eyes without eyelids let fish see underwater more easily. The scales protect the fish's body under the water.

Explain that fish do not breath air, as we do. They have gills on either side of their body which take the air out of the water for them.

Get a good book on fish from your library and show the different features of fish which protect them from their enemies: certain colors or the ability to change colors, false or giant eye marks to confuse them, etc. Two excellent books are *Animals that Live in the Sea* and *How Animals Hide* published by the National Geographic Society.

Explain that some fish live in salt water and some in fresh water. Talk about each.

Burt Dow, Deep-Water Man, Robert McCloskey
Fish is Fish, Leo Lionni
Fish Out of School, Evelyn Shaw
Goldfish, Herbert Zim
Swimmy, Leo Lionni
The Little Black Fish, Sammed Bahrang
The Little Spotted Fish, Jane Yolen

Mosaic Fish Picture

Cut a large fish picture out of heavy cardboard. Apply white glue to one small area at a time and have the child add popcorn, split peas, navy beans, black beans and rice to fish to make designs.

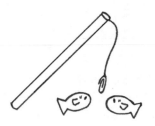

Fishing Game

Let the child "go fishing." Cut out different fish shapes 2" long from white poster board. These can be painted or colored. Tie a paper clip onto a piece of string and attach to a dowel or stick with a tack or tape (it's easier for a younger child to just use the string without the stick or dowel). You can ask the child to catch all the blue fish or the red fish to help him learn his colors.

Field Trip to View Fish

Visit a zoo aquarium or pet store to look at the fish.

Sea Jell-O®

Make Jell-O® Berry Blue gelatin as directed. When thickened, pour into a large clear serving bowl or individual bowls. Suspend gummy fish in the gelatin. Refrigerate until set. Serves 4.

Make tuna fish sandwiches.

DAY 3
SHELLS AND SHELLFISH

MATERIALS
Pictures of shells or real sea shells
Pearl, either real or fake
Snack

PROJECTS
Shell Pencil Holder: empty juice or soup can, shells, glue
Paper Plate Shellfish: small paper plates, glue, construction paper, markers

Show pictures of shells or have some for the child to hold. Tell him that these used to be houses for animals that live in the ocean. The animals make their shells out of minerals from the water. As the animals grow, so do their shells. When they die, the shells are left far behind. Let him feel the hard outsides of shells and the smooth, shiny insides.

Show him a pearl (a fake one is fine!). Explain that this was from an oyster. A little grain of sand got into the shell. To protect himself, the oyster covered the sand with secretions. The grain of sand became a pearl. Men dive deep down into the ocean to bring up oysters, hoping to find valuable pearls inside.

Explain how cultured pearls are made. Instead of a grain of sand accidentally getting into the shell, workers open the shell a tiny bit and insert a piece of sand. The resulting pearl is called a "cultured" pearl.

A House for Hermit Crab, Eric Carle
Herman, the Helper, Robert Krauss
Houses from the Sea, Alice Goudey
I Saw the Sea Come In, Alvin Tresselt
Kermit, the Hermit, Bill Peet
Seahorse, Robert A. Morse
Shells from the Sea, Robbie Trent

Shell Pencil Holder

Glue shells onto an empty juice or soup can. Use as a pencil holder. Either use your own shells or purchase some at a craft shop or import store such as Pier 1 or World Bazaar.

Paper Plate Shellfish

Make paper plate shellfish or fish. Glue small paper plates together, concave sides in. Add features with markers and glue on construction paper fins and legs.

Let the child taste shrimp or clam chowder.

CHAPTER 18
SPRING

DAY 1	WHAT IS SPRING?
DAY 2	WIND
DAY 3	RAIN

The child will learn what spring is and how wind and rain are created.

DAY 1
WHAT IS SPRING?

MATERIALS
Pictures of spring
Snack

PROJECTS
Umbrella Flower Pot: construction paper, glue
Crepe Paper Flowers: crepe paper squares, green pipe cleaners, paper
    drinking cups, rock salt or small pebbles
Crepe Paper Buds: crepe paper, small tree branch
Tissue Trees: construction paper, brown crayons, tissue paper, glue

Explain to the child that spring is a season. In spring, the world changes from winter to summer. The weather starts to get warmer, flowers come up, birds that have flown south for the winter begin to return home, the snow melts, the buds begin to swell on the trees, and the grass turns green again.

If the weather is good, take him outside to help him find some of the signs of spring mentioned above.

City Springtime, Helen Kay
Hi, Mr. Robin, Alvin Tresselt
Rabbit's Good News, Ruth Lercher Bornstein
Really Spring, Gene Zion
Spring is a New Beginning, Joan Walsh Anglund
Spring is Here!, Jane Moncure
Spring is Like the Morning, M. Jean Craig
Spring Things, Maxine Kumin
The Boy Who Didn't Believe in Spring, Lucile Clifton
Time For Spring, David Leisk
What Happens in Spring, Sandra Brooks
Will Spring Be Early?, Crockett Johnson

Umbrella Flower Pot

Cut an umbrella shape from construction paper. Glue the bottom (actually the top upside-down) to a piece of paper. Cut small flowers and leaves from brightly colored paper. Glue inside the umbrella so it looks like a flowerpot.

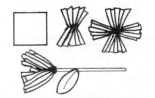

Crepe Paper Flowers

Cut squares of tissue paper; bunch up the middle. Overlap pieces going in the opposite directions, as many layers as you want. Twist bottoms together. Attach green pipe cleaners. Stand in paper cups filled with rock salt or small pebbles.

Crepe Paper Buds

Twist tiny pieces of crepe paper around a small branch to look like flowering buds. These should stay by themselves, but if your branch is too slick, you may want to glue them on.

Tissue Trees

Draw or let the child draw tree outlines on pieces of paper. Have the child color them. Glue individual pieces of tissue to the branches, so they look like spring blossoms.

Eat alfalfa or bean sprouts. These can be found canned in the oriental food section of most grocery stores or fresh in the produce department. They taste good in a sandwich with other fillings or in a pita.

DAY 2
WIND

MATERIALS
Dry tempera powder
Balloon
Facial tissue
Snack

PROJECTS
Bubble Blowing: bubble liquid (either store purchased or homemade—see recipe in Chapter 15, Day 1)
Straw Painting: soda straw, tempera paint
Pin Wheels: construction paper, straight pin or thumbtack, pencil with eraser
Paper Bag Kite: grocery bag, string, tape
Tot Kite: white paper, crayons, tape or stapler, string

On a day with a little wind, take the child outside. Have him close his eyes to see if he can feel anything tickling his face. Ask him if he knows what it is. Ask him if he can see the wind.

Put some dry powdered tempera on a piece of paper. Blow it for the child to see. Ask him what happens. Have him try.

Blow up a balloon. Ask the child what is inside. Let the air out for the child to feel. Help him understand that wind is moving air.

Hold a piece of facial tissue in one hand. Blow on it. Try to have it float in the air by blowing it upwards. Let the child try.

Talk about how the wind can be our helper. It moves the vanes on windmills, helps ships move, transports seeds, and cools us.

Anatole Over Paris, Eve Titus
Curious George Flies a Kite, H.R. Rey
Fish in the Air, Kurt Wiese
Follow the Wind, Alvin Tresselt
How Does the Wind Walk?, Nancy White Carlstrom
March Wind, Desmond Donnelly
The March Wind, Inez Rice
The North Wind and the Sun, Jean De LaFontaine
The Penguin Book of Kites, David Pelham
The Wind Blew, Pat Hutchins
The Wind Thief, Judi Barrett
When the Wind Blew, Margaret Brown
When the Wind Stops, Charlotte Zolotow
Who Took the Farmer's Hat?, Joan L. Nodset

Bubble Blowing

The child can blow with either a straw or a small funnel (dip the large end into a bubble mixture and blow out the small end). You can also use juice cans with the ends removed, coat hangers in interesting shapes, Slinkys®, or any sized hoops. Use commercial mixtures or make your own, following the recipe in the Appendix.

Pin Wheels

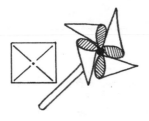

Cut 5" squares of construction paper. Cut diagonal slits from each corner nearly to the center. Fold each corner into the center. Push a straight pin or thumbtack through these center corners and attach to the end of a pencil. The child can wave the pin wheel back and forth or blow on it to make the wheel spin, or he can go outside and watch it spin with wind power.

Kites

Make a kite. Here are some simple, fun ones for a child:

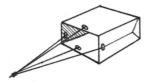

Paper Bag Kite: Draw or paint designs on a grocery bag. Punch holes at the top of each of the four sides. Tie a 16" piece of string to each hole and reinforce with tape. Join the ends. Tie a main string to this for the child to hold. This kite won't fly high, but will sail behind a running child. (This kite also works with a plastic garbage bag.)

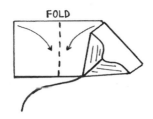

Tot Kite: Color designs on a piece of 9" x 12" lightweight paper (construction paper is too heavy). Fold in half. Bring two corners to center fold and staple or tape down. Do not crease. Turn kite over and attach a piece of string through a hole punched in the pointed end. Reinforce with tape.

Straw Painting

Do a straw painting. Pour a small puddle of bright tempera or acrylic paint on a piece of paper. Let the child make designs by blowing through soda straws.

Popcorn

Talk about how heat and air make the corn pop.

191

DAY 3
RAIN

MATERIALS
White sponge, pan and water
Rain clothes
Snack

PROJECTS
Cotton Cloud Pictures: blue construction paper, glue, cotton balls
Ink-Blot Cloud Pictures: white tempera or acrylic paint, construction paper
Sugar Pictures: colored sugar, construction paper, mister
Sponge Painting: sponge, dry tempera powder, construction paper

Hold a white sponge over a pan. Tell the child to pretend that this is a cloud. Slowly begin pouring water over it until the water begins to seep through the sponge and falls into the pan. Ask the child what this is.

Help the child understand that rain comes when the clouds are too full of water. When it falls, it seeps into the ground and "disappears" or forms puddles which evaporate back up into the sky.

Show the child rain clothes. Name each item and talk about how it keeps us dry. Have the child put on the clothes. (If you don't have rain gear, use pictures and pretend to put on the clothes.)

A Drop of Rain, Wong Herbert Yoo
All Falling Down, Gene Zion
And It Rained, Evelyn Raskin
Johnny Lion's Rubber Boots, Edith Hurd
Muddigush, Kimberly Knudson
My Red Umbrella, Robert Bright
Rain, Robert Kalan
Rain Drop Splash, Alvin Tresselt
Rain Song, Leslie Evans (helps dispel a fear of storms)
The Good Rain, Alice Goudey
The Storm Book, Charlotte Zolotow
Umbrella, Taro Yashima
When It Rains, Mary Kwitz
Where Does the Butterfly Go When It Rains?, May Garelick

Cotton Cloud Pictures

Make cloud pictures with cotton balls glued on blue paper. If you pull the cotton balls apart a little, they will look a little more like wispy clouds.

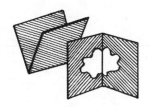

Ink-Blot Cloud Pictures

Drop blobs of white paint onto a piece of blue colored construction paper. Fold paper in half. Open and let dry. Have the child imagine what pictures the "clouds" are making.

Sugar Pictures

Sprinkle a piece of paper with either colored sugar purchased in the baking section of the grocery store or sugar you have colored with dry tempera paint powder. Set the paper out in a drizzle or spray lightly with a mister for just a minute until damp. Let dry.

Sponge Painting

Paint a picture using a wet sponge dipped in dry tempera powder.

Pudding on a Cloud

Place a large scoop of frozen or canned dairy whipped topping in a sherbet bowl. Spread the topping so that it covers the bottom and sides. Then scoop a serving of previously made instant pudding in a favorite flavor on the whipped topping. And you have pudding on a cloud.

DAY 1	WHAT ARE PLANTS?
DAY 2	WHAT DO PLANTS NEED TO GROW?
DAY 3	GROWING PLANTS

In this chapter, the child will learn about differences between plants and animals and the basic things that plants need to grow. He will also have hands-on experiences in growing plants.

DAY 1
WHAT ARE PLANTS?

MATERIALS

Forsythia or pussy willow branch
  (or other branch with buds)
Bean Seeds, paper toweling,
  plastic wrap
Snack

PROJECTS

Plant Collage: pictures from seed catalog, glue, construction paper
Flowerpots: thin colored sponges, green pipe cleaners, tape, construction
  paper, empty spools or tops from toothpaste tubes
Seed Mosaic: cardboard or poster board, glue, seeds, crayon or marker

Bring a branch from an early budding bush or tree, such as a pussy
willow or forsythia. Let the child see and feel the buds. Place in water
near the window. As leaves emerge, have him notice their size, shape,
and color.

Talk about where plants come from. A seed is a plant that hasn't started
to grow. When the seed is watered, a root starts to grow. Little roots
grow from the big root; they look like tiny hairs. They are called root
hairs. Soon a shoot pushes through the ground. Quickly the shoot turns
green. It grows toward the sun. The leaves come next. Then, flowers
follow. The flowers then make seeds, so new plants will grow next year.
(This works best for me if I draw a picture as I am talking about the seed
becoming a plant).

Alphabet Garden, Laura Jane Coats
In My Garden, Charlotte Zolotow
Jack and the Beanstalk, various authors
Mushroom in the Rain, Mirra Ginsberg
Seeds and More Seeds, Millicent Selsam
Seeds by Wind and Water, Helene Jordan
Seeds: Pop, Stick, Glide, Patricia Lauber
The Bears' Nature Guide, Stan and Jan Berenstain, pg. 42–53

From Leaves to Flowers

Here is one green leaf.   (hold up one hand cupping fingers)
And here is another.   (hold up other hand)
Soon you'll have a little flower,   (cup hands together)
To give to your mother!   (open hands up slowly like a flower)

Where Do Flowers Come From?

I will plant a little seed   (pretend to hold a seed)
In the ground so deep   (pretend to plant a seed)
I will water it so the seed   (pretend to water it)
Will no longer sleep.
Roots down, stem up   (put fingers down, then arms up)
It grows every hour.
Then one day I look
And I see a flower.   (cup hands together like a flower)

Bean Seeds

Place several bean seeds between moistened sheets of paper toweling. Cover with plastic wrap to keep the moisture in. Place in a dark place. As the week continues, show the child the root appearing. Fill small paper cups with soil or use root cups from a garden store and plant these seeds. Watch the plants grow over the next month (transplant outside or into a larger pot).

Plant Collage

Make a collage of pictures cut from a seed catalog.

Flowerpots

Make tiny flowerpots. Cut 2" pieces of colored sponges into flower shapes. Stick onto green pipe cleaner stems. Cut leaves from construction paper and attach with tape. Place in empty painted spools. Even smaller flowerpots can be made from the tops of toothpaste tubes filled with modeling clay. Cut out tiny flower sponges and attach directly to the toothpaste top.

Seed Mosaic

Make a picture out of different kinds of seeds such as bean, corn, radish, and sunflower. Have the child draw a design onto a piece of cardboard or poster paper; place the seeds on and glue in place.

Eat alfalfa sprouts in a salad or make a bean salad.

Toasted sunflower seeds

DAY 2
WHAT DO PLANTS NEED TO GROW?

MATERIALS
Celery, food coloring
House plant (optional)
Snack

PROJECTS
Carrot Plant: carrot, wet gravel or vermiculite, small plastic tub
Soil Picture: construction paper, glue, potting soil
Pressed Flowers: small flat flowers or petals, waxed paper, ribbon

Place a stalk of celery into a glass containing water you have colored with red or blue food coloring. In just a few minutes, the celery will begin to absorb the colored water through the veins. Talk about how this is the way a plant takes in the food it eats, through the "veins." You may want to relate this back to Chapter 6, Day 2, Leaves, when you talk about leaves in fall.

Show the child a house plant you've allowed to dry out. Talk about the wilted leaves. Water it. Let the child see throughout the day how the leaves become firmer and stronger (this will also work with a wilted piece of celery, if you don't have a house plant).

Show the child how a plant will grow towards the sunlight. If you don't have any indoor plants, take the child outside to look at the flowers and plants. Plants growing in a shady spot are the easiest to use as examples.

Blue Bug's Vegetable Garden, Virginia Poulet
Green is for Growing, Winifred Lubell
Let's Grow Things, Deborah Manley
The Plant Setter, Gene Zion
The Tiny Seed, Eric Carle
The Turnip, A. Tolstoy

Water the Flowers

When the flowers are thirsty	(hold hands out like flowers)
And the grass is dry,	(hold hands out flat)
Merry little raindrops	
tumble from the sky.	(fingers patter)
All around they patter	(tap fingers on table)
In their happy play,	
Till the little sunbeams	(circle arms above head)
Chase them all away.	(wave hands good-bye)

A Growing Flower

The sun comes out and shines so bright	(arms above head)
Then we have a shower.	(wiggle fingers down like rain)
The little bud pushes with all its might.	(push arms up)
And soon we have a flower.	(open hands like a f lower)

198

Carrot Plant

Cut about two inches off the top of a carrot which still has its leaves attached. Place the top on about ¾" very wet gravel or vermiculite in a small margarine tub. The water should be kept level with the bottom of the carrot. Soon, it will become a plant.

Soil Picture

Using glue as a pencil, "draw" a flower outline, or just a simple design, on a piece of paper. Sprinkle loose potting soil over it. When dry, shake off the excess soil to reveal the original picture.

Pressed Flowers

Place small flowers or petals from larger flowers between pieces of waxed paper. (The flowers from spring-blossoming trees are nice). Cover the waxed paper with a paper towel and iron on low heat. Cut to make bookmarks. Punch a hole in the top of each bookmark and attach a ribbon.

Eat vegetables and talk about how they grow from plants.

DAY 3
GROWING PLANTS

MATERIALS
Snack

PROJECTS
Terrarium: large jar or bowl with top, gravel or small rocks, charcoal, potting soil, small household plants
Eggshell Garden: egg carton, eggshell halves, potting soil, seeds (herbs, such as chives, or marigolds are good ones), plastic wrap
Avocado Plant: avocado seed, toothpicks

This day is an activity day. Tell the child that you will be spending the time making his own garden. You can choose from one or more of the following activities.

Grandpa's Too Good Garden, James Stevenson
Let's Grow a Garden, Gyo Fujikawa
The Carrot Seed, Ruth Krauss
The Little Red Flower, Paul Tripp

Terrarium

Make a terrarium out of a large glass bowl or jar with a lid (glass canisters are nice). Sprinkle in a layer of gravel or small rocks, a layer of charcoal, then about two inches of fine soil. Plant several small household plants in the soil. A small glass figurine is nice to add, too. Mist with water and replace the lid. If the sides become too humid, the lid can be opened for an hour or so. If the plants are too dry, spray once or twice with a spray bottle on mist setting.

Planting Flowers

Purchase plants or flowers and plant outdoors for the summer. The child might like to have his own plot to care for.

Eggshell Garden

Cut the top off an egg carton. Place rinsed, dried eggshell halves into each compartment. Fill each eggshell half with a small amount of soil. Add a few seeds to each shell (herb seeds such as chives or marigolds work well). Dampen soil thoroughly. Cover with plastic wrap to keep the soil moist. Place the carton in a warm, dark place until the seeds begin to sprout. Then remove the wrap and place in the sun. When tall enough, the plants can be planted in the garden—eggshell and all.

Avocado Plant

Avocado plants are easy to start, too. Poke toothpicks through the sides of the seed. Suspend the seed in a glass of water with the flat side on the bottom, just touching the water. Keep in light, but out of direct sunlight, until roots begin to form. Then move the plant into sunlight. When tap root is 4–5 inches long, transplant the avocado to a pot of soil. In about a month, a shoot will appear (it takes a long time!) When the plant is 2 ft. tall, pinch off the tip, and it will become a bushy house plant.

Greenhouse Field Trip

Visit a local greenhouse, florist, or botanical gardens to view the many kinds of plants and flowers.

Eat avocados or tomatoes.

Make an avocado dip and eat with potato or corn chips.

DAY 1	WHAT IS EASTER?
DAY 2	RABBITS
DAY 3	LET'S HAVE AN EASTER PARTY

In this chapter, the child will learn about the Easter holiday and traditional activities associated with it. He will learn more about colors as he matches eggs by color and identifies colors. He will also have the opportunity to plan and hold an Easter party for his family or friends.

Easter in the Christian world is the celebration of the resurrection of Jesus Christ, and everyone handles this differently in relationship to the "Easter Bunny" and the secular trappings of Easter. This chapter will only involve the nonreligious side of Easter. In our family, we do talk about the bunny who pays his visit to our home on Saturday. We then continue the rest of the holiday in religious worship. As with Christmas, feel free to handle this in the best way for your family.

DAY 1
WHAT IS EASTER?

MATERIALS

Easter basket, Easter grass,
  colored real or plastic eggs
Construction paper eggs and
  rabbits
Snack

PROJECTS

Easter Cards: construction paper, glue, old cards or Easter wrapping paper
Egg Cards: construction paper, gummed reinforcements
Eggshell Easter Nests: blown egg, tempera or watercolors, Easter grass or
  cotton balls, yellow construction paper, glue

Bring an Easter basket, either a special family basket or a purchased one, and let the child put Easter grass and colored or plastic eggs into it. Explain that the secular celebration of Easter has many pagan roots—it is a festival of spring and the rebirth of life in the plant and animal worlds.

(You will want to reword this in the best way for your child to understand.)

Cut out colored eggs and rabbits from construction paper and have the child match them by color. As an extra reinforcement, ask him to bring you the "blue egg" or the "green rabbit."

Hide paper eggs throughout the room. Let the child see how many he can find and put into his basket.

Chickens Aren't the Only Ones, Ruth Heller
Golden Egg Book, Margaret Brown
Jennie's Hat, Ezra Keats
Lillies, Rabbits and Painted Eggs, Edna Barth
Peter Cottontail, Karen Lee Schmidt
The Egg Tree, Katherine Milhous
The World in the Candy Egg, Alvin Tresselt
Where's My Easter Egg, Harriet Ziefert

My Rabbit

My rabbit has two big ears   (hold up middle and index fingers)
And a funny little nose.   (join the other three fingers for nose)
He likes to nibble carrots,   (wiggle the three fingers)
And he hops wherever he goes.   (move your hand up and down)

Easter Cards

Make Easter cards for friends or relatives. Pictures can be colored on paper and made into cards. Or use old cards you've saved or pictures cut from Easter wrapping. Have the child glue them onto a card made from construction paper.

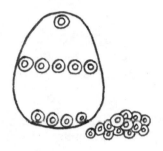

Egg Cards

Egg-shaped cards are fun to make, too. Cut an egg from colored construction paper and let the child decorate it with gummed reinforcements (available at an office supply store). Children love to lick, and they can make lots of designs.

Eggshell Easter Nests

Blow out the contents of an egg by cutting a small hole in one end and a little larger hole in the other. Blow in the smaller hole and the liquid egg will come out the larger hole. Run water through the egg to rinse it out and carefully cut off the top third with a pair of scissors. Paint with tempera or watercolors. Fill the egg shell with Easter grass or cotton balls. Cut a little chicken out of yellow construction paper and sit it in the nest.

Make a stand out of a five inch circle slit from an outside edge to the middle. Cut an inch circle out of the center, form into a cone, and glue or tape.

Any snack using eggs.

DAY 2
RABBITS

MATERIALS
Construction paper bunny
Real bunny (optional)
Snack

PROJECTS
Twirly Bunny: heavy paper or construction paper
Heart Rabbit: pink construction paper, marker, glue
Egg Rabbit: large plastic egg, wiggly eyes, felt, poster board, broom straws, cotton ball tail, glue
Paper Rabbit: large piece (18" x 24") of construction paper or poster board, crayons.

Cut a paper bunny into pieces and, one at a time, put each piece out onto the table adding the ears last. You can also do this with a blackboard or piece of drawing paper and draw each piece at a time. Let him guess what it is.

Bring a real bunny to visit. Perhaps you have a friend or neighbor who can bring in their pet (if not, most pet stores have pet rabbits at Easter time that you can go and see).

Talk about rabbits—how soft their fur is, how their long ears help them hear well, what big back legs rabbits have with smaller front ones to help them jump and run quickly, and the things that rabbits like to eat (fruits, vegetables, grass, etc.).

Have the child pretend he is a bunny. Have him hop around and wiggle his nose, if he can.

A Rabbit Has a Habit, Jane Moncure
Bunches and Bunches of Bunnies, Louise Matthews
Carrot Nose, Jan Wahl
Here Comes Peter Cottontail, Steve Nelson
Home for a Bunny, Margaret Brown
Humbug Rabbit, Lorna Balian
Max books, Rosemary Wells
Mother Rabbit's Son Tom, Dick Gackenbach
Rosebud, Ludwig Bemelmans
Snuggle Bunny, Nance Jewell
The Adventures of Little Rabbit, retold by Janet Fulton
The Runaway Bunny, Margaret Wise Brown
The Tale of Peter Rabbit, Beatrix Potter
The Velveteen Rabbit, Margery Williams
The Country Bunny and the Golden Shoes, DuBose Heyward

This Little Bunny

(begin by holding hand up)
This little bunny has two pink eyes.　　　　(bend down fourth finger)
This little bunny is very wise.　　　　　　(bend down third finger)
This little bunny has fur so white.　　　　(bend down second finger)
This little bunny will hop out of sight.　　(bend down index finger)
This little bunny's ears bend and sway.　　(bend down thumb)
Five little bunnies who hop and play.　　　(extend thumb and fingers
　　　　　　　　　　　　　　　　　　　　　back out straight and have
　　　　　　　　　　　　　　　　　　　　　them jump around)

Funny Bunny

Here's a bunny with ears so funny.　　　　　　(two fingers up and bent)
Here's his hole in the ground.　　　　　　　　(make circle with thumb and
　　　　　　　　　　　　　　　　　　　　　　　index finger of other hand)

When a noise he hears, he pricks up his ears.　(straighten fingers)
And jumps in the hole in the ground.　　　　　(jump bunny into the circle)

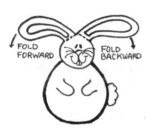

Twirly Bunny

Make a twirly bunny out of heavy paper or construction paper and let
the child color it. Fold one ear forward and one back. Have the child
stand on a chair or at the top of your stairs and let the bunny twirl down.
If he is big enough to climb a slide at a playground, he can also drop the
bunny from the top.

Heart Rabbit

Make a rabbit out of different-sized hearts cut from pink construction
paper.

Egg Rabbit

Make an egg rabbit, using a large white plastic egg. Glue on wiggly eyes.
Cut ears from felt and glue to poster board, so they will stand up.
Whiskers can be made from broom straws or stiff twine. Add a cotton
ball tail.

Paper Rabbit

Have the child color a large (18" x 24" piece of paper) rabbit picture. This can be used on Day 3 to play "Pin the Tail on the Bunny" using cotton ball tails with tape to secure.

Easter Bunny Buns

Prepare the dough from a hot roll mix as directed on package. Take a 12" x 1" strip of dough and overlap the ends to form two circles and ears. Add a small ball for the tail. Let rise until double. Bake at 375° about 12 minutes. Frost with a powdered sugar and milk glaze. Add raisin eyes.

Cookie Rabbits

Make rabbit cookies using three slices of refrigerator cookie dough: two round ones for the head and body, and one round one sliced in half for the ears. Add raisin eyes. (Save some of these cookies for the party on Day 3)

Use a cookie cutter to make bunny cookies. (Save some for the party on Day 3)

Eat carrots and lettuce like rabbits do.

DAY 3
LET'S HAVE AN EASTER PARTY

MATERIALS
Snack

PROJECTS
Bunny Ears: pink construction paper
Pin the Tail on the Bunny: large colored bunny from Day 2, cotton balls, tape
Coloring Eggs: hardboiled or blown eggs, egg dye
Bunny Egg Bag: lunch bag, markers, pipe cleaners or soda straws, tape
Margarine Tub Basket: white or pink construction paper, plastic margarine tub, pipe cleaner, handle, cotton ball
Milk Carton Basket: 8 oz. milk carton, cotton balls, glue, white cardboard, pink felt, wiggly eyes, pompom nose, florist wire or pipe cleaners

Today is a party day. Again, remember that this day will be more fun if there are several children involved. Here are some activities that you can do:

Make a rabbit basket to hold Easter candy. Fill with colored tissue paper (this is a lot less messy around the house than Easter grass!). The following are three ideas:

Bunny Egg Bag

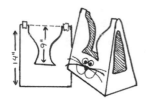

Take a lunch bag 14" long, measure down 9", and draw a line across the bag. Draw curved lines from the two corners down to this line. Make round eyes, a triangle nose, and a curvy mouth. Whiskers are pipe cleaners or soda straws bent in half and taped on. With the bag still closed, cut the ears along the lines you've drawn. Tape the tops of the ears together.

Margarine Tub Basket

Cut a bunny head pattern, as shown, out of white or pink construction paper. Have the child color on features. Glue onto the side of a plastic margarine tub (the 8-oz. size is best). Punch holes with a paper punch on the two opposite sides. Attach a pipe-cleaner handle with paper fasteners. Add a cotton ball tail.

Milk Carton Basket

Cut the top off an 8-oz. milk or whipping cream carton, leaving the sides two inches high. Glue cotton balls all around the outside. Add 3" ears cut from white cardboard and lined with pink felt. Make the face with wiggly eyes, a pompom nose, pink felt tongue, and florist wire or pipe cleaner whiskers.

Bunny Ears

Make bunny ears for each child by stapling long pink ears cut from construction paper to a headband. Sing or play the record, "Here Comes Peter Cottontail." The children can hop around to the music. Or teach them how to play musical chairs.

Pin the Tail on the Bunny

Using the picture from Day 2 , play "Pin the Tail on the Bunny," and have the children attach cotton balls with tape stuck onto the back.

Coloring Eggs

If you would like, you can color eggs—either hardboiled or blown. The new coloring tablets available in commercial Easter egg dying kits that dissolve in cold water are safer for children than using the boiling water recipe on the back of a food coloring box.

Have an Easter egg hunt using the colored eggs just made and cookies from Day 2.

Jellied Easter Eggs

> 2 pkg. fruit-flavored gelatin
> 2 pkg. unflavored gelatin
> 3 c. water
> 12 blown eggs

Using a sharp knife, carefully break egg shells so that only the tip of the shell is broken. Remove the egg. (Use the eggs themselves for breakfast). Rinse shells well with water and drain. Stir gelatins together in saucepan, add water, stir to blend. Heat to boiling, stirring until completely dissolved; set aside to cool. Place empty shells in an egg carton and fill with gelatin mixture, using small funnel or spoon (you may have to enlarge the original hole). Chill at least 3 hours or until well set. Roll eggs gently on a table to crack shells; peel carefully. Refrigerate.

Bunny Cake

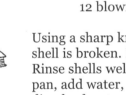

Divide one prepared cake mix between two 8" or 9" round pans. Cool completely and cut as shown. Frost all sides. Assemble on a cookie sheet or large rectangular tray. Frost top. Sprinkle with about 2 ½ c. coconut, gently pressing into frosting. Place 2–3 drops red food coloring in a bowl or jar with a lid, add ¾ c. coconut. Shake until evenly mixed. Sprinkle inside ears and bow tie. Decorate face with colored candies and red licorice. (If your child doesn't like coconut, the bunny will be fine with just white frosting and tinted pink frosting for the ears and bow tie.

Eat cookies from Day 2.

In this chapter, the child will learn about the general characteristics of insects and also specific information about butterflies, ants and bees, since they are found everywhere.

DAY 1
WHAT ARE INSECTS?

MATERIALS

Pictures of insects

Snack

PROJECTS

Tootsie Roll Caterpillars: tootsie rolls or marshmallows, pipe cleaners, toothpicks, miniature chocolate chips

Egg Carton Caterpillars: egg carton, pipe cleaners, yarn or string, marker

Show pictures of many kinds of insects. Ask what they are. Help the child learn the names of more familiar ones: ant, bee, ladybug, butterfly, caterpillar.

Talk about the things all insects have in common: six legs, one pair of antennae, a body divided into three parts, a waterproof body. Most have big eyes made up of many little ones. Most have wings. They hatch from eggs or larvae. (Adapt this information to the age of your child).

Talk about the way their bodies are colored and shaped to help them hide: walking sticks look like tree twigs; grasshoppers are green like grass; some butterflies have large "eye spots" on their wings to scare their enemies; measuring worms (sometimes called inch worms) look like little twigs.

Tell the child that even though insects sometimes look scary, they are very interesting when we look closely at them. Butterflies have many lovely colors. Some beetles have different numbers of spots on their backs. Help him learn to study the insects he sees, being careful to stay away from those that might hurt him, such as bees.

If you picked up or saw any cocoons last fall, you might want to mention this now. The butterfly or moth may even have hatched by now.

Although spiders are not really insects, you may want to talk about them here.

Spiders are like insects in many ways. They are about the same size. They have skinny, pointed legs. They have a tough covering on them to protect them. But they are different from insects, too. Spiders have eight legs rather than six. Insects have feelers, but spiders don't. Spiders only have two parts to their bodies, and insects have three. All spiders are meat-eaters and generally eat insects. They spin beautiful webs to trap their food.

A Book of Bugs, Haris Pelie
A First Look at Insects, Millicent Selsam
Anansi, the Spider, Gerald McDermott
Blue Bug series, Virginia Poulet
Buzz! Buzz!, Juan Wijngaard
Charlotte's Web, E.B. White
Chickens Aren't the Only Ones, Ruth Heller (this includes good information on insects)
Fresh Cider and Pie, Franz Brandenberg
Grasshopper in the Road, Arnold Lobel

Let's Look at Insects, Harriet Huntington
Look at Insects, Rena K. Kirkpatrick
The Bears' Nature Guide, Stan and Jan Berenstain, pp. 40–41
The Grasshopper and the Ants, retold by Margaret Wise Brown
The Grouchy Ladybug, Eric Carle
The Very Busy Spider, Eric Carle
The Very Quiet Cricket, Eric Carle
Where's That Insect?, Barbara Brenner and Bernice Chardiet (a
    Hide and Seek Science book)

Eeensy, Weensy Spider (fingerplay and song)

Eeensy, Weensy Spider climbed up the waterspout.
    (Your fingers walk up the child's arm)
Down came the rain and washed the spider out.
    (Fingers pattern rain coming down)
Out came the sun and dried up all the rain.
    (Hold arms in a circle)
So the Eeensy, Weensy Spider went up the spout again.
    (Fingers walk up again)

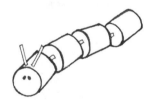

Tootsie Roll® Caterpillars

Make caterpillars using Tootsie Roll® sections or little marshmallows,
hooked together with toothpicks. Use miniature chocolate chips for eyes
and toothpicks for antennae.

Egg Carton Caterpillars

Make caterpillars from three sections of the bottom of an egg carton,
connected with yarn or string. Add pipe cleaner antennae and marker
eyes. You can add another section of three attached with yarn to make a
centipedé.

Eat your Tootsie Roll® or marshmallow caterpillars.

Ants on a Log

Fill a stalk of celery with peanut butter. Dot the peanut butter with
raisins (ants).

MATERIALS
Butterfly pictures

PROJECTS
Butterfly Clothespins: tissue paper squares, wooden clothespin, glue, pipecleaner
Butterfly Kite: drinking straws, glue, construction paper, kite string

Show a picture of a butterfly. Point out the eyes, body, antennae, and wings. Mention that there is a special dust on butterfly's wings that helps it fly.

Discuss the differences between butterflies and moths: butterflies usually fly in the daytime—moths at night; butterflies rest with their wings up—moths with their wings flat; butterflies have slender bodies— moths are plump and often look furry; butterflies have slender antennae—moths' antennae look like feathers.

ABC Butterflies, Marcia Brown
Creepy, Crawly Caterpillars, Margery Facklam
Open House for Butterflies, Ruth Krauss
Our Caterpillars, Herbert Wong and Matthew Vessel
The Butterfly Collector, Naomi Lewis
The Butterfly, A. Delaney
The Butterfly, Paula J. Hogan
Very Hungry Caterpillar, Eric Carle

Butterfly Clothespins

Select several different colors of tissue paper and cut into 6" squares. Pinch them together and glue inside the slot of an old-fashioned clothespin. Cut a pipe cleaner in half and glue each piece onto the top for antennae.

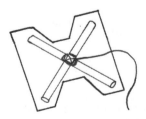

Butterfly Kite

Make a butterfly kite. Cross two drinking straws and glue together in the middle. Tie a two foot piece of string to the straws where they cross. Lay onto a sheet of paper and cut out as shown. Color the paper, so that it looks like a butterfly. Glue the straws to the paper. Hold onto the string and fly your kite.

Butterfly Sandwiches

Make butterfly sandwiches. Make a sandwich with the child's favorite filling. Cut the bread diagonally in both directions to form four triangles. Cut a carrot into one long and two short strips for the body and antennae. Place on a plate with the sandwich "wings" along the side.

DAY 3
ANTS AND BEES

MATERIALS
Books on ants and bees
  Snack

PROJECTS
Ant Farm: 2 jars which fit inside each other, sand, sugar, plastic wrap
Beehive: Styrofoam® egg, gold giftwrap cording, straight pins, glue, tiny bee or
  flower decoration
Beeswax Candle: beeswax, candle wicking or string (all available at craft stores)

Ants: Talk about how they live in colonies and work together as a group. Most of the ants are worker ants. They gather food and take care of the queen and baby ants. They are females, but do not lay eggs. Only the queen lays eggs. Soldier ants guard the nest. They have bigger and stronger jaws than the other workers.

Bees: Like ants, bees work together as a group. Bees live in hives. There is only one queen in a hive who lays the eggs. Male bees are called "drones" who mate with the queen. Most of the hive is made up of worker bees which are female bees. The workers gather nectar for honey and pollen. Some make honeycomb wax out of their bodies to store the honey, some take care of the queen, some feed the baby bees, some fan the air, some keep the hive clean and some guard the hive. A few baby bees are fed a special food called royal jelly. Eventually, they become queens. When a young queen bee grows up, the old queen leaves with many workers to make a new hive.

Ants are Fun, Mildred Myrick
Bees, Wasps and Hornets, Robert M. McClung
Buzz, Buzz, Buzz, Bryon Barton
Follow Me, Cried Bee, Jan Wahl
Here Come the Bees!, Alice Goudrey
Honey Bees, Jane Lecht (a National Geographic Young Explorer book)
Honey Bee's Busy Day, Richard Fowler
Little Lost Bee, Joan Kapral
The Ant and the Elephant, Bill Peet
The Ants Go Marching, Berniece Freschet
The Honey Bee and the Robber, Eric Carle

The Bee Hive

Here is the hive   (hold hands together to make a hive)
But where are the bees?
They're hiding inside   (pretend to look inside)
As quiet as you please.
Now look at the bees coming out of the hive.
1, 2, 3, 4, 5.   (hold up fingers one at a time)
Buzz!!

Ant Farm

Make an ant farm in a jar. Place a small, clean, glass jar upside-down inside a large, clean, glass jar (this keeps the ants confined around the outside of the glass, so you can see them). Fill the space between the jars with sand or soil. Locate some ants and make an ant trap by mixing a little sugar and water in a small jar and laying it on its side near an ant hill. When you have about 20 ants, place them inside the large jar and cap it or cover with plastic wrap. In a day or two, the ants will begin to build tunnels. Once a week, feed the ants a few drops of sugar-water and maybe a few grains of bird or grass seed. Don't overfeed the ants. Keep the jar at room temperature away from the heat and fairly shaded.

Beehive Pin Holder

Make a beehive pin holder. Cut the bottom off a Styrofoam® egg (available at craft stores), so it will stand upright. Make a small hole in the top of the egg. Insert the end of a gold giftwrap cord, narrow macramé cord, or gold sewing braid; glue and secure with a pin. Apply glue to top section of egg and begin wrapping cord in spiral. Apply more glue as each section is covered. Decorate finished hive with artificial flowers or a tiny bee.

Beeswax Candles

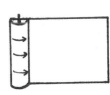

With a pair of scissors cut a sheet of beeswax 3–4" long. Place a length of wick down on one end, letting it stick out about ½". Roll the wax very lightly until the candle is the desired thickness. The finished thickness depends upon the size of your holder.

Feeding the Ants

Go outside and feed the ants. Take very small pieces of different kinds of food (crackers, bread, cookie crumbs) and put them by where you see ants. Watch the ants discover the food and begin to carry it away. Come back an hour later and see how much is gone.

Make honey candy or taffy. Here's an easy recipe:

> 2 c. honey
> 1 c. sugar
> 1 c. cream or evaporated milk

Combine ingredients and cook slowly to hard ball stage. Pour onto buttered platter, and when cool enough to handle, grease or butter hands and pull until the taffy turns a golden color. Cut into pieces.

DAY 1	WHAT IS A FARM?
DAY 2	WHAT DO FARMERS DO?
DAY 3	FARM ANIMALS

In this chapter, the child will learn about farms and why they are important to us. He should be able to identify various farm animals and their role in our lives.

DAY 1
WHAT IS A FARM?

MATERIALS
Farm pictures

PROJECTS
Box Barn: shoe box, red and white tempera paint, red poster paper, tape
Block Barn: wooden blocks

Show a picture of a farm. Ask the child what it is. Help him learn the names for the farmhouse, barn, fences, and chicken coop.

Help the child learn where the different animals sleep on the farm. For example, the horses and cows sleep in the barn, the chickens in the chicken coop, the pigs in houses in the pigsty, and the sheep in a field or fenced area.

Big Red Barn, Eve Bunting
Big Red Barn, Margaret Wise Brown
Blue Barns, Helen Sewell
Bright Barnyard, Dahlov Ipcar
Grandpa's Farm, James Flora
I Know a Farm, Ethel Collier
Little Farm, Lois Lenski
Over the River and Through the Woods, Lydia Child
The Barn, John Schoenharr
The Year at Maple Hill Farm, Alice and Martin Provensen
Tim Mouse Visits the Farm, Judy Brook
Wake Up, Farm, Alvin Tresselt

Box Barn

Make a barn. Paint a box, shoe size or larger, with red tempera paint. A red triangle from poster paper can be taped on one end to make a false loft. Use white paint to outline a door and loft windows. The double door can be cut open as shown (we will make the animals on Day 3).

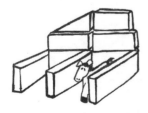

Block Barn

With blocks, build a barn. Small blocks can be used to make partitions (stalls) for the imaginary horses and cows.

Eat hard boiled eggs, fruits, or vegetables, talking about how they come from a farm.

220

DAY 2
WHAT DO FARMERS DO?

MATERIALS
Pictures of farmers
Snack

PROJECTS
Butter: ½ pint heavy whipping cream

Talk about the jobs a farmer does: planting, hoeing, feeding the animals, milking the cows, gathering eggs, mending fences, pitching hay, etc. Have the child pantomime these different activities.

Talk about the tools farmers use. Try to have a picture of a tractor. Have the child try to guess what the farmer is going to plant with the tractor. Talk about other tools generally found on farms (pitchforks, a harvester, hay baler, etc.).

Farmer Barnes and the Goats, Joan Cunliffe
Farmer in the Dell, illustrated by Diane Zuromskis
Farmer Palmer's Wagon Ride, William Steig
If I Drove a Tractor, Miriam Young
Old MacDonald Had a Farm, Tracey Campbell Pearson
Rock-a-Bye Farm, Diane Johnston Hamar
Rooster's Off to See the World, Eric Carle
The Little Farmer, Margaret Brown
Who Took The Farmer's Hat?, Joan L. Nodset

The Farmer in the Dell

The farmer in the dell; the farmer in the dell;
Hi, ho, the derry, oh, the farmer in the dell.
The farmer takes a wife; the farmer takes a wife;
Hi, ho, the derry, oh; the farmer takes a wife.

(Continue singing adding a child, a horse, a cow, etc.)

Old McDonald Had a Farm

Old McDonald had a farm, E-I-E-I-O.
And on this farm he had a cow, E I E I O.
With a moo-moo here, and a moo-moo there,
Here a moo, there a moo, everywhere a moo-moo,
Old McDonald had a farm, E-I-E-I-O.

(Continue singing adding a pig—"oink, oink"; a sheep—"baa, baa"; etc.)

Little Boy Blue, Come Blow Your Horn (verse)

Little Boy Blue, come blow your horn.
The sheep's in the meadow,
The cow's in the corn.
Where's the little boy who looks after the sheep?
He's under the haystack, fast asleep.

Farm Field Trip

Visit a farm to watch what the farmer does. If you don't know a farmer, a drive in the country will allow you to pass buy farms where you can talk about what you see from the road on a farm.

Dairy Field Trip

Visit a dairy to watch the cows being milked.

(Note: Look in the phone book for dairies to see if you can arrange a visit)

Butter

Make butter from heavy whipping cream by whipping it with an electric mixture until it begins to solidify; serve on bread.

DAY 3
FARM ANIMALS

MATERIALS
Pictures of farm animals
Snack

PROJECTS
Animal Book: white paper, animal stickers or pictures of farm animals cut from magazines
Farm Animals: cardboard or poster board, white paper, crayons

Show pictures of farm animals and tell something about each one. Help the child learn the sounds the animals make (use pigs, cows, sheep, horses, ducks, geese, goats, chickens, and roosters).

As you hold up the picture of an animal, have the child tell you what it is. Go through the pictures again and have the child tell you the sound that each one makes.

Talk about the food that comes from each animal.

A Pile of Pigs, Judith Ross Enderle
Barn Dance!, B. Martin, Jr. and J. Archambault
Barnyard Banter, Denise Flemming
Farm Animals, An "Eye-Opener" book
Farmyard Animals, Jean Wilson
Friendly Farm Animals, Esther Meeks
Have You Seen My Duckling?, Nancy Tafuri
Horses, Janusz Grabiarski
Horses, Margaret Brown
Little Chick, Lisa McCue
Little Chick's Big Adventure, Richard Fowler
Look at a Calf, Dave Wright
Look at a Colt, Dave Wright
One Horse Farm, Ipcar Dahlov
Our Animal Friends, Alice and Martin Provensen
Petunia series, Roger Duvoisin
Pig, Horse, or Cow, Don't Wake Me Now, Arlene Alda
Sherman the Sheep, Kevin Kiser
Small Pig, Arnold Lobel
The Chicken Book, Garth Williams
The Little Duck, Judy Dunn
The Little Goat, Judy Dunn
The Little Lamb, Judy Dunn
The Story of a Little Red Rooster, Berta and Elmer Hader

Mary Had a Little Lamb

Mary had a little lamb,
Little lamb, little lamb.
Mary had a little lamb
Whose fleece was white as snow.

Baa, Baa Black Sheep
(sung to the same melody as "Twinkle, Twinkle Little Star")

Baa, baa, black sheep
Have you any wool?
Yes sir, yes sir.
Three bags full.

One for my master,
One for my dame,
And one for the little boy
Who lives in the lane.

Baa, baa, black sheep,
Have you any wool?
Yes, sir, yes, sir,
Three bags full.

Farm Animal Book

Have the child glue stickers or cut out pictures of animals on pages of a little paper book (see Chapter 2 for instruction on making paper books). The child can also draw pictures directly on the pages.

Farm Animals

Color little pictures of farm animals. Mount on cardboard. Cut half circles from cardboard for stands. Make a slit halfway down. Cut a corresponding size in the base of the picture. When placed at right angles, the picture will stand (see illustration). Have the child put the animals in and around the barn you made on Day 1.

Eat food from farm animals: eggs, milk, bacon, etc.

CHAPTER 23
THE ZOO AND WILD ANIMALS

DAY 1	WILD ANIMALS
DAY 2	ELEPHANTS
DAY 3	THE CAT FAMILY
DAY 4	MONKEYS
DAY 5	BEARS
DAY 6	THE ZOO

In this chapter, the child will learn about wild animals and specific characteristics of more familiar wild animals. The chapter will culminate with a study of and a field trip to a zoo for a hands-on experience.

MATERIALS
Pictures of wild animals

PROJECTS
Paper Book: white paper, stickers or pictures of wild animals
Lotto Game: white poster board, animal pictures or stickers
Animal Puzzles: animal picture or drawing, white poster board or
    construction paper, spray adhesive

Show pictures of many familiar wild animals such as elephants, monkeys, lions, tigers, giraffes, bears, zebras, and crocodiles. Help the child learn the animals' names. Briefly talk about each one discussing its shape, size, color, and habitat.

Play an animal guessing game. Hold up a picture and have the child tell you what it is. Then display all the pictures, name one, and have the child point to it.

Play animal charades. Imitate an animal and have the child guess what it is. After a while he will want to do this and have you guess.

About Animals, Richard Scarry
Animal Babies, Harry McNaught
Animal Babies, Max Zoll
Animal Babies, Ylla
Animals Everywhere, Ingrid and Edgar D'Aulaire
Animals, Anno
Animals, Lois Lenski
Crictor, Tomi Ungerer
Grabianski's Wild Animals, Janusz Grabianski
Henry Explores the Jungle, Mark Taylor
In the Forest, Marie Ets
In the Jungle, Eugene Booth (a Raintree Spotlight Book)
Jungle Animals, an "Eye Opener" book
The Big Book of Wild Animals, Felix Sutton
The Camel Who Took a Walk, Jack Tworkov
What Do You Do with a Kangaroo?, Mercer Mayer
Wild Animals: From Alligator to Zebra, Arthur Singer

Animal Paper Book

Make a paper book (see general directions in Chapter 2). Have the child glue pictures cut from magazines, lick stamps, or place stickers of wild animals onto the pages.

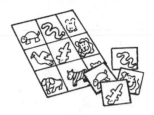

Animal Lotto

Make a lotto game. On pieces of cardboard 9" square, draw lines dividing each piece into nine 3" squares. Using stickers or hand-drawn pictures attach a picture of a different animal on each square. Cut 3" square cards; glue corresponding pictures to them. Draw the cards one by one and have the child try to match the pictures on the cards with their pictures on the larger squares.

Animal Puzzles

Have the child color animal pictures (coloring books are good sources). Cover the back with spray adhesive and press down on a piece of construction paper or light cardboard. Cut into about five large pieces. Have the child try to put the picture back together again.

What a great day for animal crackers!

MATERIALS
Picture of an elephant
Snack: peanuts

PROJECTS
Soda Straw Elephant: construction paper, soda straw, crayons, tape
Pencil Holder: empty soup can, gray paper, crayons, or wiggly eyes

Hold up a picture of an elephant. Ask the child what it is.

Talk about the different parts of the elephant and what they are used for:

Trunk: picking up objects, picking up food, filling with water for a bath or a drink.

Ears: big and floppy; African elephants have bigger ears than Indian ones.

Tusks: used by the elephant for protection; made of ivory.

Legs: large and strong and important to help support the elephant.

Tough hide: protection from insects and the jungle.

Talk about what elephants eat. They are plant eaters, gathering grass with their trunks and digging up roots with their tusks. They can also drink up to 50 gallons of water a day.

Ah-choo, Mercer Mayer
Babar the Elephant series, Laurent and Jean de Brunhoff
Baby Elephant series, Sesyle Joslin
Did Anyone See My Elephant?, Robert Leydenfrol
Elmer, David McKee
Horton Hatches the Egg, Dr. Seuss
If I Rode an Elephant, Miriam Young
Little Elephant, Arthur Gregory
Little Wild Elephant, Anne Michael
"Stand Back" said the Elephant, "I'm Going to Sneeze", Patricia Thomas
The Ant and the Elephant, Bill Peet
The Elephant Who Wanted to be a Leopard, Eve Witte
The Elephant's Visit, Bob Bauer
The Smallest Elephant in the World, Alvin Tresselt

March to a record (the "Elephant Patrol" from the **Jungle Book** movie by Walt Disney is a good one) imitating elephants. Clasp hands together in front and bend from the waist, swinging arms back and forth like a trunk. Walk slowly with heavy steps.

Elephant Pencil Holder

Make an elephant pencil holder. Cover an empty soup can with gray paper. Add paper ears and a trunk. Color on eyes or glue on wiggly eyes.

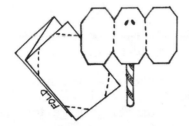

Straw Elephants

Make elephants on straws. Fold a piece of construction paper into thirds, cut small triangles off the top two sides and larger triangles off the bottom. Open up and draw eyes on center section. Tape a soda straw to the back. When the child holds on to the straw and waves it up and down, the elephant's ears will flop.

Eat peanuts like the elephants in the zoo.

DAY 3
THE CAT FAMILY

MATERIALS
Pictures of lions, tigers and
    other cats

PROJECTS
Lion Container: empty juice or shortening can, gold, felt, yarn, glue, wiggly eyes

Talk about the wild members of the cat family: lions, tigers, leopards, jaguars, and others (we will be talking about tame ones in the next chapter).

Show pictures and help the child tell the difference between the various cats. The colors will be the biggest difference he will notice.

Talk about the things that wild cats have in common (even with house cats): padded paws, appetites for meat, whiskers which act as feelers, excellent hearing and sight, nocturnal habits (hunt at night), eyes to help them see in the dark.

The tiger is the biggest "cat." Tigers are striped to help them hide in tall grass. They are found in Asia.

Another familiar "cat" is the lion. It lives in Africa and is called the "King of Beasts" because of its regal mane.

A Painted Tale, Kate Canning
Here Come the Lions, Alice Goudey
Hubert's Hair Raising Adventure, Bill Peet
Johnny Lion series, Edith Hurd
Leo, the Late Bloomer, Robert Kraus
Lion Cubs, a National Geographic Young Explorer book
The Happy Lion series, Louise Fatio
The Rat and the Lion, Jean de LaFontaine
The Sleepy Little Lion, Margaret Brown
The Story of Little Black Sambo, Helen Bannerman
The Terrible Tiger, Jean Prelutsky
The Tiger Hunt, Mary Villarejo
Tigers in the Cellar, Carol Fenner

Lion Container

Make a lion container. Cover an empty juice can with gold felt. Around the edges of the top, glue small pieces of yarn for the mane. Cut a circle of felt the size of the can lid for the face and glue over yarn. Use pipe cleaners for the whiskers. Glue on "wiggly" eyes. Cut a piece of yarn for the tail and glue on the bottom. This also may be made with a shortening can and used to hold crayons.

DAY 4
MONKEYS

MATERIALS
Monkey pictures
Snack

PROJECTS
Jumping Monkey: white paper, cardboard or poster board, paper fasteners, tongue depressor, marker, tape or glue
Monkey Mask: paper plate, string or yarn, tempera paint

Show pictures of monkeys. Have the child tell you what they are.

Talk about the things that monkeys do. They use their tails to swing from trees, use their fingers to pick fruit and peel it, and live together in groups.

Talk about what monkeys eat: fruits and vegetables.

Have the child act out being a monkey.

Arthur series, Russell Hoban
Babar and Zephir, Laurent deBrunhoff
Caps for Sale, Esphyr Stobkina
Cecily G. and the 9 Monkeys, H.A. Rey
Curious George series, H.A. Rey
Five Little Monkeys, Juliet Kepes
Five Little Monkeys Jumping on the Bed, Eileen Christelow
Five Little Monkeys Sitting in a Tree, Eileen Christelow
Jacko, John S. Goodall
Little Gorilla, Ruth Bornstein
Monkey Tale, Hamilton Williamson
Run Little Monkeys, Run, Run, Run, Juliet Kepes
The Monkey and the Crocodile, Paul Galdone

Jumping Monkey

Draw a monkey picture as shown. Cut out and glue to cardboard. Join pieces loosely with paper fasteners. Tape or glue a tongue depressor behind the head. When you bounce the depressor up and down, the monkey will "jump."

Monkey Mask

Make a monkey mask out of a paper plate. Cut to fit the child's head. Paint or color appropriate colors. Let the child pretend to be a monkey.

Peanuts or bananas

Peanut butter and banana sandwiches

DAY 5
BEARS

MATERIALS
Pictures of bears

PROJECTS
Teddy Bear Picnic: teddy bears, celery, peanut butter, raisins, bread and honey
Climbing Bear: wood or cardboard, string, 6" dowel

Show a picture of a bear. Ask the child what it is.

Show pictures of different kinds of bears and talk about where they live. Polar bears live in northern climates. Brown and black bears live in mountain forests. You might also want to talk about koalas and pandas; even though they aren't really bears, everyone calls them bears (koalas live in Australia and pandas live in China).

Talk about what bears eat: bugs, berries, honey, and sometimes meat.

Talk about what bears do in the winter: hibernate (sleep). You might want to refer back to Chapter 12, Winter, where we first talked about hibernation.

Bears have big appetites, and bears in zoos often do tricks to get something to eat. They can be trained to dance and perform in circuses, because they can stand on their hind legs.

A Bargain for Francis, Russell Holmes
A Pocket for Corduroy, Don Freeman
Ask Mr. Bear, Marjorie Flack
Bear Hugs, Joe Alborough
Berenstain Bears series, Stan and Jan Berenstain
Beware the Polar Bear, Miriam Young
Brimhall series, Judy Delton
Buzzy Bear series, Dorothy Marino
Corduroy, Don Freeman
Gideon, the Little Bear Cub, Emma Mora
Goldilocks and the Three Bears, various authors
Little Bear series, Else Minarik
Little Polar Bear, Hans de Beer
Milton the Early Riser, Robert Kraus
Mr. Bear and the Robbers, Chizuko Kuratomi
Nobody Listens to Andrew, Elizabeth Guiloile
Not This Bear!, Berniece Myers
Paddington series, Michael Bond
Pandas, Donna K. Grosvenor (a National Geographic Young Explorer book)
Penguins and Polar Bears, Sandra Lee Crow (a National Geographic Young Explorer book)
Playful Pandas, a National Geographic Action book
The Bear Who Had No Place to Go, James Stevenson
The Bear's Toothache, David McPhail
The Bear, Raymond Briggs
The Lazy Bear, Brian Wildsmith
The Marshmallow Caper, Gloria Miklowitz
Where's My Teddy?, Jez Alborough
Winnie the Pooh, A.A. Milne

Teddy Bear Picnic

Take a favorite teddy bear or bears on a picnic in a park or just in your own backyard. Be sure to bring lots of bear food—ants on a log (see recipe below), bread and honey, nuts and raisins, and dried fruit.

Climbing Bear

Make a climbing bear as shown. Cut two bears out of cardboard. Cut two pieces of string 3' long and attach with tape to a 6" dowel or piece of coat hanger. Glue the two bears together leaving a channel for the string to run through the arms as shown (make sure that the channel runs at an angle as illustrated or the bear will not actually climb). Tie a string to the middle of the dowel. When the string is held by one person or hung over a door knob, the bear will "climb" as the strings are pulled (you can also make a wooden version of this bear. Use only one pattern and drill holes for the strings).

Honey on bread

Ants on a Log
Spread celery pieces with peanut butter and dot with raisins (ants).

Nuts, raisins, and dried fruit

DAY 6
THE ZOO

MATERIALS
Zoo pictures
Snack

PROJECTS
Animal Box Zoo: small boxes, white paper, crayons or markers
Animal Masks: paper plates, tempera paint or crayons, string
Egg Carton Critters: egg cartons, glue, construction paper, tempera paint

Talk about what a zoo is—a place where many animals are kept, so we can go and see them.

In many zoos today, the animals are not kept in cages behind bars but in simulations of their natural environments. They are separated from the people by deep gullies, wire fences, or water. This is nice for the animals because they can feel more at home in a zoo, and we can see them doing many of the things they would do if they were out in the wild.

Talk about the rules of a zoo, e.g. don't feed the animals unless the zoo allows it; don't lean over partitions or climb fences; don't throw things at the animals.

Again, review the names of many animals by showing the pictures and having the child say the names.

Cecily G. and the 9 Monkeys, H.A. Rey
Come to the Zoo, Ruth M. Jansen
Crictor, Tomi Ungerer
George and Martha series, James Marshall
Goodnight Gorilla, Peggy Rathmann
Hugo the Hippo, Thomas Baum
I Met a Penguin, Frank Asch
If I Ran the Zoo, Dr. Seuss
My Visit to the Zoo, Aiki
One Day at the Zoo, Dick Snyder
Something New at the Zoo, Esther Meeks
The Giant Giraffe, Eve Holmquist
There's a Hippopotamus Under My Bed, Mike Thaler
We Visit the Zoo, Bruce Wannamaker
What Do You Want With a Kangaroo?, Mercer Mayer
What If a Lion Eats Me and I Fall in a Hippopotamus' Mud Hole?, Emily Hanlon
"You Look Ridiculous," said the Rhinoceros to the Hippo, Bernard Waber
Zoo Animals, Leonard Shorall
Zoo Babies, Donna K. Grosvenor (a National Geographic Young Explorer book)
Zoo City, Stephen Lewis

Animal Zoo
Draw animal pictures on the sides of small boxes. Arrange the boxes in groups to form a zoo.

 **Animal Masks**

Make animal masks out of paper plates like the monkey mask in Day 4. Have the child act out the animal as he wears its mask.

 **Egg Carton Critters**

Cut egg cartons into animal shapes. Paint with tempera paint. Add construction paper legs and wiggly eyes. Here are two ideas—use your own.

 **Field Trip to the Zoo**

Visit a local zoo. If you don't have one, perhaps there is a petting farm or a "traveling zoo" in your area you can arrange to see.

 Again have a box of animal crackers.

DAY 1	DOGS
DAY 2	CATS
DAY 3	OTHER PETS

The child will study two familiar pets, dogs and cats. He will also be exposed to information about other pets that people enjoy.

MATERIALS
Pictures of dogs
Snack

PROJECTS
Doggie Mobile: brown construction paper, string or yarn, black buttons, black and white crayons

Show pictures of different kinds of dogs (libraries have lots of books).

Talk about the sizes of dogs. Talk about the colors and the different kinds of hair in their coats.

Talk about what dogs do to help people: collies and sheep dogs help shepherds take care of their sheep; retrievers and other hunting dogs help hunters find and capture game and wild birds; St. Bernards are used to find lost climbers; German Shepherds help the police and blind people; etc.

Talk about the kind of food that dogs eat. Make a point of helping the child understand that "people food," especially sweets, are harmful to a dog.

Talk about the other things that must be done to take care of dogs: giving them water, providing a place for them to sleep, taking them to a vet to get their shots to protect them from disease, making sure they get enough exercise, brushing their coats, and having their hair trimmed as needed.

Claude, the Dog, Dick Gackenbach
Dogs, Camille Koffler
Go Dog Go, P.D. Eastman
Harry the Dog series, Gene Zion
Pete's Pup: 3 Puppy Stories, Syd Hoff
Pretzel, Margret and H. A. Rey
Puppies, Judith E. Rinard (a National Geographic Young Explorer book)
Spot books, Eric Hill
The Big Book of Dogs, Felix Sutton

Doggy Mobile

Fold a piece of brown paper in half and cut as shown. Open up and hang down two black button eyes and a brown paper nose. Attach a string to the top and hang from doorway or ceiling.

Pet Store Field Trip

Visit a pet store and look at the dogs. Talk about the different breeds.

Visit a Friend's Dog

If you don't own a dog, arrange a visit with a friend who does. Have them show you where their dog sleeps, what he eats, and other aspects of his life.

Make sugar cookies or cut slices of bread in the shape of dog bones. Let the child pretend that he is a dog eating his dinner.

MATERIALS
Pictures of cat
Snack

PROJECTS
Origami Cat: lightweight paper
Spool Cat: empty spool, cardboard, crayons, glue

Handle this day much as you did in Day 1, Dogs. Talk about what clean animals cats are, because they are always grooming themselves. Cats are easy to care for, since they can look after themselves better than most pets.

Talk about the purring noises cats make when they are happy or contented. Talk about the cat's paws and how the claws can be extended for protection (to scratch another animal or climbing a tree).

Talk about what cats eat. Farmers like to have cats around their barns to catch mice and rats. Cats also like to catch birds, which makes many people unhappy.

Cat Trap, Molly Coree
Cat, You Better Come Home, Garrison Keillor
Catch that Cat, Gernando Krahn
Cats, Camille Koffler
Convent Cat, Barbara Willard
Find the Cat, Elailne Livermore
Grandmother Lucy's Cat series, Joyce Wood
Katy's Kitty: 3 Kitty Stories, Syd Hoff
Kittens for Nothing, Robert Kraus
The Big Book of Cats, Gladys Cook
Where's That Cat?, Barbara Brenner and Bernice Chardiet

Two Cats of Kilkenny (verse)

There once were two cats of Kilkenny.
Each thought there was one cat too many.
So they fought and they fit,
And they scratched and they bit
Till, excepting their nails
And the tips of their tails,
Instead of two cats, there weren't any.

The Three Little Kittens (verse)

The three little kittens, they lost their mittens,
And they began to cry,
"Oh, Mother dear, we sadly fear, our mittens we have lost."
"What, lost your mittens? You naughty kittens,
Now you shall have no pie."
The three little kittens, they found their mittens,
And they began to cry,
"Oh, Mother dear, see here, see here. Our mittens we have found."
"What, found your mittens? You darling kittens,
Now you shall have some pie."

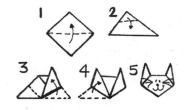

Origami Cat

Use a square piece of black construction paper. Fold as shown. Flip paper over between steps 4 and 5. Draw on face.

Spool Cat

From black construction paper, cut out the front and back of a cat as shown. Add facial features and stripes if desired. Glue to the ends of an empty spool of thread or an empty film canister.

Eat goldfish crackers.

Eat tuna fish—a favorite cat food.

Children also think it's fun to lick milk out of a saucer as kittens do.

DAY 3
OTHER PETS

MATERIALS
Pictures of various pets
Snack

PROJECTS
Parrot Puzzle: white paper, crayons, cardboard or poster board, glue
Pet Mobile: pet pictures, cardboard, string

Have the child think of some other animals his friends have as pets, such as hamsters, gerbils, mice, fish, birds, rabbits, and turtles.

Talk about each one and how we take care of it. What kind of a home does it need to stay in? What does it eat?

It's also important for the child to understand that there are many animals that aren't meant to be kept as domestic pets. Some exotic birds, hermit crabs, deer, and other animals have been harmed by removing them from their natural habitats and taking them into people's homes.

Babar and the Wully-Wully, Laurent and Jean de Brunhoff
Crictor, Tomi Ungerer
Hazel was an Only Pet, John Hamberger
Helping Our Animal Friends, Judith E. Rinard (a National
        Geographic Young Explorer book)
Let's Get Turtles, Millicent Selsam
My Goldfish, Herbert Wong
Nicholas' Favorite Pet, Inger Sandberg
Pet Show!, Ezra Keats
Polly, the Guinea Pig, Margaret Pursell
Two Guppies, a Turtle, and Aunt Edna, Lois Wyse

Parrot Puzzle

Draw a parrot picture as shown onto a piece of heavy white paper. Let the child color it as he desires, using lots of bright colors. Glue to a piece of cardboard. When dry, cut out the cardboard into 4 to 10 pieces, depending on the age of the child. Have him practice putting the pieces back together.

Pet Mobile

Draw pictures of a bird, a turtle, a snake, a fish, and a rabbit. Have the child color them. Attach to a mobile, as shown in Chapter 2.

242

Pet Store Field Trip

Visit a pet store and have the child see other kinds of pets that some people own. Or, if you have a neighbor or friend with an unusual pet, make arrangements for your child to visit and watch them care for their pet.

Eat crackers as in "Polly Wants a Cracker."

DAY 1	OUR EARTH
DAY 2	DINOSAURS
DAY 3	THE SUN
DAY 4	THE NIGHT SKY
DAY 5	RIVERS
DAY 6	TREES
DAY 7	MOUNTAINS

In this chapter, the child will learn about the physical properties of the world that haven't been studied yet. These will be related to those things that he has learned in previous chapters.

MATERIALS

Globe or map
Lamp or flashlight
Snack

PROJECTS

Show the child a globe. Talk about the parts that are land and the parts that are the oceans. If you don't have a globe, a map of the world will do if you explain that it's like the world cut open and laid down flat.

Discuss what lives on the land and what lives in the ocean. Be sure to relate this to the previous chapters on animals, plants, and the ocean.

Talk about what parts of the world are hot and what parts of the world are cold.

Show them how part of the world is having night when the other side if having day. This can be shown by placing the globe by a lamp in a dimly lit room—the other side will be dark.

Hailstones and Halibut Bones, Mary O'Neill
The Bears' Nature Guide, Stan and Jan Berenstain

Day Walk

Take the child on a walk. Talk about the wonderful world we live in. Help the child appreciate the many beauties of nature in your neighborhood or nearby park. Ask him about the sounds he hears, such as birds singing, dogs barking, the wind blowing the leaves, crickets chirping, etc.

Night Walk

This is also fun to repeat at night. Ask him how things look different at night than in the daytime. Ask him what sounds he hears now.

DAY 2
DINOSAURS

MATERIALS
Pictures of different kinds
of dinosaurs

PROJECTS
Fossil Molds: modeling clay, small pie plate, fossil items as suggested below,
    Plaster of Paris, paper cup, plastic spoon, paint
Dinosaur Play: play dough, small twigs, green paper, glue, small dinosaur toys
Dinoprints: empty plastic meat containers, string or yarn, small pan big
    enough for child to step into

*Because of the great interest in dinosaurs, it seemed only appropriate
to talk about these creatures in our study of the World Around Us.
There are numerous fiction books available about dinosaurs that you
can read. I have kept this day pretty factual, but you can adapt it
however you want according to the age and understanding of your
child. You may also want it to last more than one day.*

Show pictures of dinosaurs. Talk about what dinosaurs are. Dinosaurs
lived many millions of years ago. Dinosaurs had tough scaly skin with
good eyesight and hearing. They had long tails but they apparently
stood, walked and ran like ostriches. We learn these facts from studying
the fossil imprints left. Some dinosaurs had scales such as we find on
lizards today, and others had armor plates right in their skin. We don't
know what colors the dinosaurs were, but we think that they probably
had colors to help them hide, just as animals do today.

Dinosaurs laid their eggs in holes dug in the sand or in mud nests built
on the ground. They were about the size of ostrich eggs.

Plant-eating dinosaurs had blunt teeth or beaks. They were large—bigger
than school buses. The largest of these was the Brachiosaurus, a kind of
Brontosaurus. Another famous herbivore was the Stegosaurus which
had a spiked tail and two rows of bony plates down its back.

Another was the Triceratops, which had two horns on its brow and a
horn on its nose. Some of these dinosaurs ate the branches of trees,
while others ate the plants that grew on the ground.

To see how they ground their food, place some small rocks and some
green leaves into a plastic, resealable bag. With the bag between your
palms, rub your hands back and forth about 25 times. Look at the leaves.
They will be crushed, just as the dinosaurs would have crushed them
while eating them.

Meat-eating dinosaurs had very sharp teeth and claws, such as lions and
tigers today. They were built like large birds with bony tails. The Tyran-
nosaurus Rex was the largest. He was 47 feet long. To help him
understand the size of this dinosaur, you can show him what this length
is by comparison to your house or another large object. You can also go
outside and pace off 47 feet. But in spite of its size, the T-Rex had tiny
arms and 2 fingers on each hand. It lived in North America. Its teeth
were about 6 inches long.

Birds are among the few living descendants of dinosaurs today. We don't know why dinosaurs died. Maybe the earth became too cold or too hot for them.

Bones, Bones, Dinosaur Bones, Byron Barton
Dandy Dinosaurs, Better Homes and Gardens
Danny and the Dinosaur, Syd Hoff
Dinosaur Questions, Bernard Most
Dinosaur Roar, Paul and Henrietta Strickland
Dinosaur Stories, Paul Strickland
Dinosaur Story, Joanna Cole
Dinosaurs, David Lambert and Rachel Wright (this book has some excellent illustrations)
Dinosaurs and their Young, Russell Freedman
Dinosaurs for Every Kid, Janice VanCleave
Good Night Dinosaurs, Judy Sierra
If the Dinosaurs Came Back, Bernard Most

Fossil Molds

Flatten a large piece of modeling clay in a small pie plate. Press an item that you want to model firmly into the clay. Suggested items are sea shells, rough-sided nuts, leaves and pine needles, or small plastic animals, including dinosaurs. Carefully remove the item leaving its outline in the clay. Mix Plaster of Paris in a small paper cup, ½ c. plaster to ¼ c. water. When smooth, pour mix into the mold until the crevices are filled. When the Plaster of Paris is completely dry, carefully remove the clay and paint the plaster. This gives the child an idea of how fossils came about, and also how difficult it is to know what the whole animal, such as a dinosaur, was like from just the fossil remains. (Be sure to throw the remaining plaster mix away when hardened. Don't wash down your sink.)

You can also pour the prepared Plaster of Paris into a pie pan. Place an object covered with Vaseline into the plaster mixture (Don't push too deeply or immerse). When hardened, gently remove the object and paint the "fossil" imprint left inside.

Dinosaur Play

Make a large quantity of play dough (recipe in Appendix) and flatten on a cookie sheet. Have the child make hills and valleys in the play dough. Trees can be made by cutting small leaf-shaped pieces of green paper. Cover the tips of small tree branches with glue and sprinkle with the leaves. When dry, these "trees" can be placed in the play dough. The child can place his small dinosaur figures (either commercial or ones he has made with the play dough) in among the valleys and trees. If you have a sand box, this can be used instead of the play dough for larger dinosaurs.

Dinoprints

Cut a clean plastic tray from a meat package into the shape of two large dinosaur footprints. Tie string or yarn to the sides and tie on child's feet. Have him step into a pan filled with water and then walk across the sidewalk to leave his prints.

DAY 3
THE SUN

MATERIALS
Snack

PROJECTS
Tissue Rainbow Picture: black construction paper, colored tissue paper, tape
Cardboard Sundial: cardboard, sharp dowel or pencil, marker
Sun Prints: light sensitive paper, white paper, leaf or other flat object

Ask the child what is up in the sky that makes it light in the daytime (the sun).

Tell him that years ago, the people thought the sun went around the earth, but now we know the earth goes around the sun. He might like to use the word "revolve." This concept is fun to act out. You could be the sun and your child the earth or vice versa.

Talk about the sun as our friend: it heats the world, helps the plants and flowers grow, melts the snow so winter can end, heats many homes, etc.

Explain that we must be careful with the sun, though. We should never look at it, and we can't stay out too long in it, or we'll get sunburned.

Dawn, Uri Shulevitz
Follow the Sunset, Herman Schneider
Little Cloud, Eric Carle
Sun, a Wonder Starter book
Sun Up, Alvin Tresselt
The Day We Saw the Sun Come Up, Alice Goudey
The North Wind and the Sun, Jean De LaFontaine
Where Does the Sun Go at Night, Mina Ginsberg
Why the Sky is Far Away, a Nigerian Folktale

Tissue Rainbow Picture

Inside a black construction paper frame, glue strips of colored tissue paper to make a rainbow—red, orange, yellow, green, blue, purple. Tape the frame to a window. When the sun shines through the tissue paper, the colors will appear somewhere on the wall or floor of the room.

Cardboard Sundial

To help the child see the movement of the sun through the sky, make a sundial. Cut a 12" circle from cardboard. Place it flat on the ground in some sunny place. Push a sharp dowel or pencil through the center of the cardboard and into the ground, so it will stand upright. At hourly intervals, mark on the sundial where the shadow falls. The next day, you'll have a fairly good idea what time it is by looking at the place where the shadow crosses your marks.

Sun Prints

Use light-sensitive paper (we get ours at a school supply store) to make designs. Place the paper in the sun, covering part of it with another paper design or an object such as a leaf. Soon, the paper will be exposed to the sun and will change color, except where the paper has been covered (this can also be done just with dark construction paper, but it takes several days before the uncovered outside has faded enough.)

MATERIALS

Pictures of moon and stars
Two different sized balls,
   flashlight or lamp
Snack

PROJECTS

Star Sky: black construction paper, empty soup can, pin, flashlight

Ask the child what he sees when he looks up in the sky at night. Ask him where the sun has gone.

Moon: Explain to the child that the moon turns (revolves) around the earth. This is easier to understand, if you have a small ball for the moon and a larger one or a globe for the earth. Tell him that the moon gets its light from the sun's reflection. Perhaps he has seen what looks like a man in the moon. The "man" is really the shadows of huge craters or holes on the moon.

Stars: Children seem to understand best when the stars are explained as small suns far, far away. The stars were used to guide the sailors and travelers.

Show the child some pictures of the constellations. Help him imagine the pictures behind the star groups.

A Bucketful of Moon, Toby Talbot
Bears in the Night, Stan and Jan Berenstain
Go to Bed, Virginia Miller
Goodnight, Goodnight, Eve Rice
Goodnight Moon, Margaret Brown
Grandfather Twilight, Barbara Berger
Happy Birthday, Moon, Frank Asch
Look at the Moon, May Garelick
Midnight Moon, Clyde Watson
Moon Man, Tomi Ungerer
Papa, Please Get the Moon for Me, Eric Carle
Sleep Well, Little Bear, Quint Bucholz
Ten, Nine, Eight, Molly Bang
The Moon Jumpers, Janice May Udry
The Sky is Full of Stars, Franklyn M. Branley
The Sun's Asleep Behind the Hill, Mirna Ginsburg
The Way of the Stars, Ghislaine Vautier
Time for Bed, Mem Fox
Wait Till the Moon is Full, Margaret Wise Brown
What the Moon Saw, Brian Wildsmith
What's in the Dark?, Carl Memling
When I'm Sleepy, Jane R. Howard
the stories or legends behind the constellations

Wynken, Blynken and Nod by Eugene Field

Wynken, Blynken, and Nod one night
Sailed off in a wooden shoe,
Sailed on a river of crystal light
Into a sea of dew.
"Where are you going, and what do you wish?"
The old moon asked the three.
"We have come to fish for the herring fish
That live in this beautiful sea;
Nets of silver and gold have we!"
Said Wynken, Blynken, and Nod.

The old moon laughed and sang a song,
As they rocked in the wooden shoe;
And the wind that sped them all night long
Ruffled with waves of dew.
The little stars were the herring fish
That lived in that beautiful sea
"Now cast your nets wherever you wish,
Never afraid are we!"
So cried the stars to the fisherman three.
Wynken, Blynken and Nod.

All night long their nets they threw
To the stars in the twinkling foam.
Then down from the skies came the wooden shoe,
Bringing the fisherman home!
'Twas all so pretty a sail, it seemed
As if it could not be;
And some folks thought 'twas a dream they'd dreamed
Of sailing that beautiful sea;
But I shall name you the fisherman three:
Wynken, Blynken and Nod.

Wynken, Blynken are two little eyes,
And Nod is a little head,
And the wooden shoe that sailed the skies
Is a wee one's trundle-bed;
So shut your eyes while Mother sings
Of wonderful sights that be,
And you shall see the beautiful things
As your rock in the misty sea
Where the old shoe rocked the fisherman three—
Wynken, Blynken and Nod.

Twinkle, Twinkle, Little Star

Twinkle, twinkle, little star,
How I wonder what you are.
Up above the world so high
Like a diamond in the sky.
Twinkle, twinkle, little star,
How I wonder what you are.

I See the Moon (verse)

I see the Moon
And the Moon sees me.
God bless the moon,
And God bless me.

Star Sky

Glue paper stars or gold and silver sticker stars onto black construction paper.

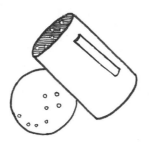

Home Planetarium

Cut open both ends of a soup can. Cut circles the size of the soup can opening out of black construction paper. Punch pin holes in the shape of familiar constellations. Hold the black construction paper circles against one soup can opening and hold a flashlight inside. Darken the room and the stars will shine up on the ceiling.

Look at the stars at night.

Night Sky Jell-O™

Make 1 package Jell-O™ Berry Blue gelatin. Pour into an 8" square pan. Refrigerate until firm. Cut into ½" cubes. Divide among four bowls. Stars: Roll a marshmallow until flat. Cut into a star shape, moisten slightly and sprinkle with yellow colored sugar. Place one or more on each bowl of Jell-O™ sky.

DAY 5
RIVERS

MATERIALS
Pictures of rivers
Snack

PROJECTS
Paper boat: heavy white paper
Raft: Popsicle® sticks, glue

Show a picture of a river or draw a picture. Ask the child where the water comes from—the earth (a spring), melting snow, rain.

Make a little "river bed" outside. Run some water from a pitcher or a hose down the trough. Point out that the water took a little dirt with it, too. Thus, the pathway has become deeper. This is called "erosion."

Talk about the difference between a brook, a stream and a river—size, how fast the water is moving, how deep it is.

Talk about how rivers help us—watering the land; providing drinks for birds and animals; providing homes for many animals, such as fish, beavers, and frogs; making power for hydroelectric plants or mills; transporting things, such as logs to the lumber mill or food to market.

Alfie Finds the Other Side of the World, Charles Keeping
All Along the River, Allan Fowler (a Rookie Read-About Science book)
The Boats on the River, Marjorie Flack
Tim Mouse Goes Downstream, Judy Brook
We Live by the River, Lois Lenski
Where the Brook Begins, Margaret Bartlett

Popsicle® Stick Raft

Glue 6 Popsicle® sticks together on a table. Glue 2 other sticks across the top and bottom for strength. Set it sail in a river or your bathtub.

Visit to a River

Visit a nearby river or stream. Talk about the many things you see, such as rocks, reeds, boats, birds, fish, and frogs.

Boat Ride

Take a boat ride on a river.

Paper Boat

Make a boat as in Chapter 13, Day 5, Boats. Watch it sail on the little riverbed you made with a hose in the introduction.

Boat Eggs

Make "boat eggs" as shown in Chapter 13, Day 5, Boats.

DAY 6
TREES

MATERIALS
Paper cutouts of a tree
Snack

PROJECTS
Pine Cone Animals: pine cones, felt, wiggly eyes, small pompom, glue
Sap Rising: celery, food coloring
Leaf Prints: leaves, construction paper, paint brush or toothbrush, tempera paint, stick
Tree Rubbings: white paper, crayon, parts of a tree, leaves, needles, bark

Have cutouts of the parts of a tree—trunk, roots, branches, leaves or needles. As you put them up on a flannel board, have the child guess what it is you are making. Help him learn the words (you can also draw the parts on a blackboard if you would prefer).

On a walk or with the help of a book, talk about what makes trees different from one another— the height, the bark, the shape and color of the leaves or needles, the seeds, pods or cones for reproducing.

Talk about the ways that trees help us—lumber to build things, fuel, shade, erosion prevention, windbreaks for protection from storms, homes for the birds and animals, cleansing the air, etc.

Talk about all the things we can do to help protect trees—don't tear away the bark which protects them; be careful not to break branches; don't dig around the trunk and break the roots; watch out for harmful insects that might destroy a tree.

A Tree is Nice, Janice Udry
Have You Seen Trees?, Joanne Oppenheim
Our Tree, Herbert Wong and Matthew Vassel
Spooky Old Tree, Stan and Jan Berenstain
The Dead Tree, Alvin Tresselt

Pinecone Animals

Make pinecone animals. Glue wiggly eyes onto a pine cone. A pompom can be the nose. A mouth and ears are cut from felt. Some suggestions are mice, reindeers (with pipe cleaner antlers), pigs, and dogs.

Sap Rising

Place a stalk of celery in colored water. The child can watch the color drawn through the stem—compare this to the way the sap rises through the tree. You might mention that we have done this before in Chapter 19 with plants. This will help him understand that trees are big plants.

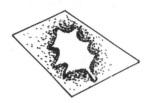

Leaf Prints

Make leaf prints. Place flat leaves onto a sheet of heavy paper. Dip a paint brush or toothbrush into tempera paint. Holding it over the paper, gently tap it against a stick and the paint will leave spatters on the paper. When dry, remove the leaf and the outline will remain on the paper.

Tree Rubbings

Make tree rubbings, using different parts of the tree—leaves, needles, bark. Place these under a piece of paper. Rub over the top with the side of a crayon. The impression of the object underneath will appear on the paper.

Have the child pretend that he is a giant. Let him eat broccoli, asparagus and celery "trees."

DAY 7
MOUNTAINS

MATERIALS
Mountain pictures
Snack

PROJECTS
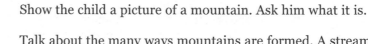
Clay Mountains: clay or playdough
Rock Animals: large pebbles, acrylic paint, construction paper, glue

Show the child a picture of a mountain. Ask him what it is.

Talk about the many ways mountains are formed. A stream can cut down the earth on either side until eventually mountain walls remain. Volcanoes can push up the earth from underneath forming a mountain. Or sometimes a volcano's lava explodes out of the ground forming a mountain. Sometimes the earth folds or parts of the rock move upward and some move downward (keep this simple and don't spend a lot of time on it.)

Talk about the animals that live on mountains—goats, coyotes, mountain lions.

Talk about the weather on mountains—colder than at lower altitudes, windy, snowy.

Bernie's Hill, Erik Blegvad
Everybody Needs a Rock, Byrd Baylor
Rocks and Minerals, Illa Podendorf
Timothy Robbins Climbs a Mountain, Alvin Tresselt

The Bear Went Over the Mountain

The bear went over the mountain,
The bear went over the mountain,
The bear went over the mountain,
To see what he could see.
To see what he could see,
To see what he could see.
Oh, the bear went over the mountain,
The bear went over the mountain,
The bear went over the mountain,
To see what he could see.

Clay Mountains

Have the child form mountains out of clay or play dough.

Mountain Drive

Walk or drive through some mountains. If you don't have mountains, try to drive through some hills and explain that they are like mountains.

Rock Animals

Make rock animals. Find some large pebbles with bumps on them which look as if they could be some kind of animal. Paint the appropriate color and add construction paper features, if necessary. We have found rocks that look like fish, dogs, mice, and turtles. If you paint them with clear varnish when done, they will stay bright and pretty.

SPECIAL HOLIDAYS
>**NEW YEAR'S DAY**
>**MARTIN LUTHER KING DAY**
>**ST. PATRICK'S DAY**
>**EARTH DAY**
>**CINCO DE MAYO**
>**MOTHER'S DAY**
>**FATHER'S DAY**

RECIPES

MUSIC

SPECIAL HOLIDAYS

Everyone handles holidays differently. This section of the book covers several that do not fit into the units of the book itself. It is up to you whether you want to use these ideas. There are several criteria which can make your holiday celebrations run smoothly without a lot of work on your part.

- Choose a color scheme for your celebration. Besides the traditional red and green for Christmas or orange and black for Halloween, make the colors a part of your child's memories. For instance, fuchsia, purple, gold, and silver are great colors for New Year's. Green is, of course, for St. Patrick's Day; browns and greens for Earth Day; and yellow, oranges, and reds for Cinco de Mayo. I always buy paper napkins that go along with the holiday, using our regular plates and cups.

- Choose food that you will traditionally serve on this day. We always have a cherry pie dessert for Washington's birthday, green pancakes for St. Patrick's Day breakfast, and hamburgers for Mother's Day (I think that this is because it is something my husband can cook!) This is even more meaningful if it is something that you or your husband did when you were children.

- Find a special story or book and always read it on that special day.

- Have special decorations that you put up every time. Perhaps you have a picture of Martin Luther King or Lincoln or a plaque with a leprechaun on it. Many stores sell plastic decorations that will stick to windows for the various holidays. Have the child put these up. Crepe paper, twisted and strung from a dining room or kitchen light to the four outside walls, adds a festive air with little time or trouble. Balloons are also great, too. We have a red plate that we always use for the birthday boy or girl.

The important thing is to make your holidays fun and full of traditions. Following are the extra holidays that we celebrate and what we enjoy doing.

NEW YEAR'S DAY

The first day of January every year is celebrated as New Year's Day. Since ancient times, people have celebrated the first of the new year. In Switzerland, the people dressed up in masks and costumes. In China, they light fireworks. In the Netherlands, everyone is invited to open houses. In Scotland, they sing a song called "Auld Lang Syne." (You can sing this to the child if you know it).

We always celebrate New Year's Eve with our children. I make special food they wouldn't eat at other times of the year. We have blowers and hats we wear. We bang on pans. When the children were younger, we would secretly set the clocks ahead several hours, so the children could enjoy the countdown until the new year, without having to stay up until it really was midnight.

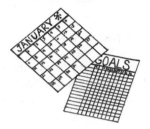

On New Year's Day, we give each child a calendar for the coming year. We mark special events such as birthdays and holidays on it and help them use it during the year. There are many calendars out just for children. They can mark off the days and put on stickers for special events.

We also make goals for the new year. Each child decides what they want to accomplish during the coming year, and we write them down on their own chart. For pre-schoolers, these may be such things as learning to write their name, learning to make their bed, helping set the table at night, tying their shoes, etc. Every month we review their goals and talk to them about how they can achieve them. On New Year's Day, we look at their old goals and praise them for the things they were able to do during the past year.

MARTIN LUTHER KING DAY

For many children, the celebration of Martin Luther King Day is not an important factor in their life until they enter school. For this reason, this day is in the Appendix of the book to be included in your studies as you desire.

The fact that Martin Luther King, Jr., was murdered is also something that you might want to avoid talking about. You can tell the child that Dr. King died in 1968.

Martin Luther King, Jr., was an African-American leader who was born in Atlanta, Georgia, over 70 years ago. When he was growing up, African-American children and white children weren't allowed to go to school together. African-American people had to ride at the back of buses. They couldn't even drink out of the same drinking fountains. When they went out to a restaurant, they couldn't eat in the same part of the restaurant as the other people.

When Martin Luther King, Jr., grew up, he became a minister. As he tried to help people who were sad or sick, he realized that it was important for African-Americans to be equal to whites. But he wanted people to do this through peace and not through fighting. He spoke to people all over the country to ask them to change the laws, so African-American people could do the same things that white people could do. Because of his hard work, those laws were passed and now it doesn't matter what color skin a person has, he can still be like everyone else.

When he died, people wanted to honor him every year on his birthday. So they made a holiday on the third Monday of January to celebrate all that he did to help his people.

Talk to the child about people he knows who are different than he is—Hispanics, Native Americans, and others, as well as African-Americans. Talk about the fact that we shouldn't make people who aren't like us feel sad, because we aren't kind to them. You might even apply this to handicapped people as well if it would be appropriate.

Happy Birthday, Martin Luther King, Jean Marzello (a great book which tells of Dr. King's life with well-drawn pictures)

What is Martin Luther King Day?, Margot Parker (an interesting mixture of cartoon illustrations and real photographs)

Martin Luther King, Jr. Day, Dianne M. MacMillan (narrative is too difficult for pre-schoolers, but it is a good supplemental book)

ST. PATRICK'S DAY

Tell the story of St. Patrick. Hundreds of years ago, when Patrick was sixteen, he was stolen from his father's farm in England by raiders from Ireland. He had to tend sheep. During this time, he prayed a lot for help. When he was 22, he ran away, took a ship to Europe and spent many years studying there. After a few years, he heard a voice telling him to return to Ireland to teach them about the Catholic religion. He spent many years studying and became a monk. When he returned to Ireland he spent many years traveling around teaching the people about the Christian religion. He tried to change the old holidays and combine them with Christian customs. The people always honored their gods with spring fire rites, so Patrick had the people have bonfires at Easter time.

When he died the people mourned for twelve days. He had not only taught the people, but he had written down the history of the people. His name is found all over Ireland in the names of towns and villages, such as Kirkpatrick, Kilpatrick, etc.

St. Patrick's Day is on his death, March 17th. It was also thought to be the first day of spring. People started wearing a shamrock to represent the three members of the trinity of Catholic faith.

Today in the United States, there are more people of Irish descent than there are in Ireland.

Children love hearing about leprechauns. Leprechauns are little bearded make-believe men. They wear green suits and caps. The leprechaun's job is to work day and night mending the shoes of other fairies. Supposedly, they are rich and mean. If you capture one, he is supposed to give you his pot of gold in order to escape. They, along with shamrocks, are one of the symbols of St. Patrick's Day.

Talk about lucky charms—horseshoes, rabbit's feet, four-leaf clovers, etc.

Gilly Gilhooly: A Tale of Ireland, Arnold Brogeen and Patrick Lynch
Leprechauns, Legends & Irish Tales, Hugh McGowan (more than
    you'll ever want to know about St. Patrick's Day!)
Little Bear Marches in the St. Patrick's Day Parade, Janice
traditional Irish fairy tales

Hunting for the Green

Take a walk through your house and have the child show you everything he can find that is the color green. You can count the items as you go along and see how many he can find.

Treasure Hunts

Hide gold coins (at party stores and candy stores, you can buy little ones that are chocolate) and have him search for them.

Hide Lucky Charms® and have him hunt for them.

Shamrock Cupcakes

Place paper muffin cups inside a muffin pan. Put three marbles into the pan between the paper cup and the edge. (See illustration.) Pour a white or yellow cake batter into the paper cup and bake. When done, carefully remove the cupcakes from the pan. They will have a shamrock shape which can be frosted with green frosting.

Prepare anything green. We have green colored pancakes and milk for breakfast. The night before, empty an undrained can of pears into a bowl and add several drops of green food coloring. They will be green by the morning. Finger Jell-O® (recipe in Appendix) can be made with green gelatin. Have lime flavored drinks. Also any dish with potatoes—even french fries—would be in keeping with this holiday.

EARTH DAY

On April 22, the people of the United States celebrate Earth Day. For many years, this day was celebrated as Arbor Day. In recent years, this celebration was changed to the last Friday in April. Earth Day was made to remind us about taking care of our world. This might be a good day to plant a tree or shrub in your yard. This is also a good day to review the discussion about recycling that you had in Chapter 14.

Remind the child about cleaning up litter and garbage. Walk through your neighborhood with a garbage bag and pick up litter.

This is an interesting club that you can write to for more information including membership:

Kids for Saving Earth Club
P.O. Box 47247
Plymouth, MN 55447-0247

CINCO DE MAYO

On May 5, Cinco de Mayo, have a fiesta to celebrate Mexican Independence Day. Have red, white and green (the colors of the Mexican flag) decorations. Eat Mexican food. Make a piñata following the directions in Chapter 11, Day 5, Christmas in Other Lands.

About 80 years ago, a woman wanted the country to have a holiday to honor mothers. This day is always held on the second Sunday in May. Because this lesson will probably be taught by the mother, you may want to have the father or someone else work with the child to make a gift for his mother.

It would also be nice if he would like to make a card or a gift for grandmothers. (Yes, I know that they know celebrate grandparents day in September, but I feel this is just one more opportunity for the card and flower companies to sell merchandise. If you want to celebrate then, feel free to adapt these and the Father's Day ideas to the child's grandparents.)

I have tried to include several different ideas that could be used to celebrate this day:

Breakfast in Bed

What mother wouldn't enjoy breakfast in bed? It is easy for a child to fill a bowl with cereal. Precut bananas and strawberries could be placed on top to make a face. These can also be used as decorations on top of frozen or fresh made pancakes or waffles. Dad will be needed for this one!

Finger-painted Hand Card

Fold a piece of construction paper in half. "Paint" the child's palm and fingers with acrylic paint. Have him open his hand wide and place the hand flat on construction paper. You will probably have to press down on the fingers, so that the paint will cover the area properly. Immediately, wash off their hand in warm soapy water, so that the paint doesn't end up in the wrong place! The adult can write "Happy Mother's Day," the child's name (if he can't write it himself) and the date on the card.

Coupon Books

Make a coupon book for Mommy. Cut construction paper into fourths and write a promise on each page. The child can color them if desired. Have the child give the ideas of what he would like to do. Some suggestions might include things that the child can do such as set the table, water the plants, fold the napkins, play with the baby, and give a hug and a kiss.

Pudding

Pour 2 c. milk in a 1 qt. glass jar. Add a small package of Mommy's favorite instant pudding. Screw on the top. Shake for two minutes until pudding is well mixed and pour into bowls.

FATHER'S DAY

Father's Day is celebrated on the third Sunday in June. You might want to talk to your child again about all the things that daddys do. Serve Dad's favorite foods.

Dad T-shirt

Using idea for Mother's Day card, paint the child's hand with fabric paint and place it face down on a man's T-shirt that has been prewashed and dried. Put a piece of aluminum foil inside so the paint won't bleed through to the back. When the paint is dry, write the child's name on the hand print with a black permanent marker. If you have several children, these hand prints can be done in different colors, one for each child.

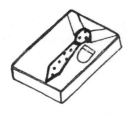

Coupon Books

See under Mother's Day. Ideas for Dad might include shining (not polishing) shoes, dusting his dresser, hugs and kisses, and getting him the paper to read.

Dad Shirt Cake

Make Dad's favorite cake in a 9" x 13" cake pan. When the cake is cool, leave inside pan or remove to a plate. Frost with a white or pastel frosting. Outline the tie, collar, and pocket with contrasting frosting.

Cookie Dough

1 c. margarine, softened
1 ½ c. sugar
2 eggs
1 T. orange juice

1 T. orange rind, optional
½ tsp. baking soda
½ tsp. salt
4–5 c. flour

Cream margarine and sugar; beat in eggs. Sift together dry ingredients and add to creamed mixture. Add rind, juice and vanilla. Chill. After rolling and cutting out cookies, bake on an ungreased cookie sheet at 350° for 8 minutes. (This keeps a long time in the refrigerator. Or divide in fourths, put in freezer bags and freeze. Allow to thaw for about 1 hour at room temperature.)

Finger Jell-O®

4 envelopes powdered gelatin mixed with 3 small pkg. Jell-O®
4 c. boiling water

Mix until gelatin is dissolved. Place in 9" x 13" pan. Chill until set. (Can also just use 4 small or 2 large pkgs. Jell-O®, mixed with 2 ½ c. boiling water.)

Frosting

½ c. margarine, softened
1 egg yolk

1 tsp. vanilla or other flavoring
4–5 c. powdered sugar

Beat margarine and egg yolk together. Add vanilla. Add powdered sugar, 1 c. at a time, beating well until frosting is desired consistency. Drops of food coloring can be added if desired. This will store well in a covered bowl in the refrigerator.

Fruit Salad

1 c. crushed pineapple, drained
1 c. mandarin oranges, drained
1 c. sour cream

1 c. coconut
1 c. miniature marshmallows

Mix together and refrigerate for several hours or overnight.

Giant Kiss and Marshmallow Treat Nest

¼ c. margarine 3 c. miniature marshmallows
5 c. Rice Crispies®, corn flakes or chow mein noodles (for Giant Kiss you can also use a chocolate rice crispie cereal such as Cocoa Pebbles®)

Melt margarine and marshmallows over low heat. Remove from heat and stir in rice cereal. Let it cool a little and shape into small bird nests or follow directions for Giant Kisses. You may have to butter the child's hands, so he can form the nest more easily.

Honey Taffy

2 c. honey 1 c. sugar
1 c. cream or evaporated milk

Combine ingredients and cook slowly to hard ball stage. Pour onto buttered platter, and when cool enough to handle, grease or butter hands and pull until the taffy turns a golden color. Cut into pieces.

Ice Cream (this is a very easy recipe)

2 14-oz. cans sweetened condensed milk
1 2-liter bottle or 5 12-oz. cans carbonated beverage, any flavor

Ice Cream Freezer Method: in large bowl, combine ingredients and pour into ice cream freezer. Freeze according to manufacturer's instructions.

Refrigerator-Freezer Method: in large bowl, combine ingredients. Turn into 9" x 13" pan, freeze to a firm mush, about 1 hour. Break into pieces and turn into large mixer bowl. Beat until smooth. Return to pan; cover. Freeze until firm.

Macaroon Treat Nest

1 can sweetened condensed milk (not evaporated)
1 14-oz. package coconut (5 1/3 c.)
2 tsp. vanilla

Mix well. Place spoonfuls onto cookie sheet. Make indentation in center. Cook 10–12 min. at 350°. This is such a soft cookie that you may need to make the indentation again after it is finished baking. Quickly move to a cooling rack.

Play Dough

1 c. flour	1 T. oil
½ c. salt	1 T. vanilla
1 T. alum	food coloring
1 c. water	

Mix dry ingredients. Add oil, water and coloring. Cook over medium heat, stirring constantly until it reaches the consistency of mashed potatoes. Remove from heat. Add vanilla. Store in a plastic bag.

Popcorn Balls

½ c. margarine	2 c. brown sugar
1 c. corn syrup	1 can sweetened condensed milk
1 quart popcorn	

Cook on medium heat until mixture comes to a boil. Boil for five minutes. Remove from heat and add a can of sweetened condensed milk. When cool, pour over 1 quart of cooked popcorn. Shape into popcorn balls the size you would like to have.

Pretzels

¾ c. warm water	2 c. flour
1 pkg. yeast	½ tsp. sugar
½ tsp. salt	For final cooking, ½ egg, Kosher salt

Add yeast to water, stirring until dissolved. Add salt and sugar; stir. Add flour and stir until mixed. Knead very lightly on floured surface until completely smooth. Store in greased container with plastic wrap on top, for a least one hour or overnight. Punch dough down. Divide into 16 equal portions. Shape into pretzels (or whatever shape you are talking about that day) and place on aluminum foil-lined cookie sheet. Brush with egg, sprinkle lightly with Kosher salt. Bake at 425° for 15 min.

Salt Dough

1 c. cornstarch	1 c. salt
¾ c. water	

Combine starch and salt in a saucepan. Add water and cook over low heat, stirring constantly until ball forms. Let cool and keep in plastic bag. Take out only as much as you will need. Add food coloring, drop by drop, and knead with hands until it is colored evenly. This will dry after a day. If you do not color the dough, it can be painted after dry with tempera paints.

Soap Bubbles

2 c. warm water

6 T. Dawn® dish washing liquid

6 T. glycerin (find at drugstores)

dash sugar

Mix well. Let stand in an open container at least one day before using. The child can blow with either a straw or a small funnel (dip the large end into the bubble mixture and blow out the small end). You can also use juice cans with the ends removed, coat hangers bent into interesting shapes, or any size hoops.

Vegetable Soup (this is an "un-recipe"— you have to make it to taste)

Cut up whatever vegetables you wish: carrots, potatoes, summer squash, green peppers, celery, onions to equal about 4 c. Cook with just enough water to steam. Season to taste with 3–4 cubes chicken bouillon. Add milk to the proportion that you like, bring to simmer. This can be thickened by adding 3 T. cornstarch, mixed with 1 c. water—add little by little until it's the thickness you like.

Head, Shoulders, Knees & Toes

Head, shoul-ders, knees & toes. Knees & toes. Knees & toes.

Head, shoul-ders, knees & toes. Eyes, ears, mouth & nose.

If Your're Happy

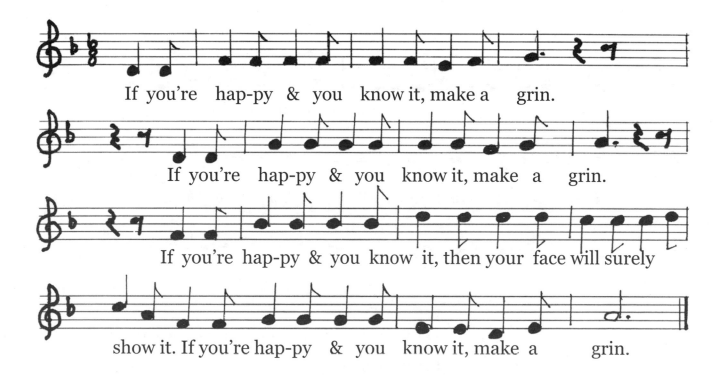

If you're hap-py & you know it, make a grin.

If you're hap-py & you know it, make a grin.

If you're hap-py & you know it, then your face will surely

show it. If you're hap-py & you know it, make a grin.

2. If you're sad & you know it make a frown.

3. If you're sleepy & you know it make a yawn.

4. If you're angry & you know it make a scowl.

Bright Leaves

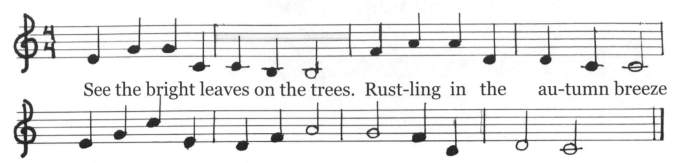

See the bright leaves on the trees. Rust-ling in the au-tumn breeze

Whir-ling, twir-ling through the air, Fall here and there.

Five Little Pumpkins

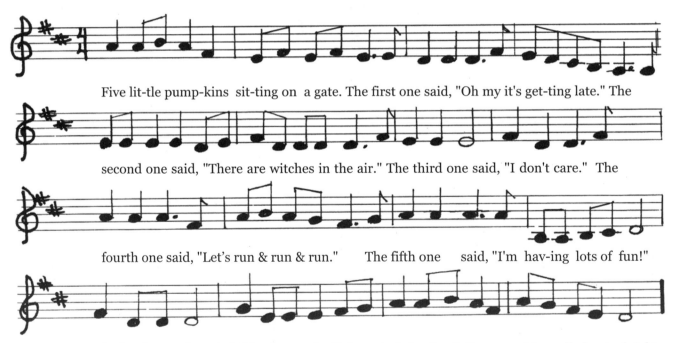

Five lit-tle pump-kins sit-ting on a gate. The first one said, "Oh my it's get-ting late." The

second one said, "There are witches in the air." The third one said, "I don't care." The

fourth one said, "Let's run & run & run." The fifth one said, "I'm hav-ing lots of fun!"

"Whoo" went the wind. "Out" went the lights. And the five little pump-kins rolled out of sight.

Five Little Pilgrims (you will have to adapt the song's rhythm a little)

Five little Pilgrims on Thanksgiving Day.
The first one said, "I'll have potatoes if I may."
The second one said, "I'll have turkey roasted."
The third one said, "I'll have chestnuts toasted.
The fourth one said, "Oh, cranberries I spy."
The fifth one said, "I'll have some pumpkin pie."
"Mmm" went each mouth. "Ah" went each tummy.
And the five little pilgrims thought the food was yummy.

Dreidel Song

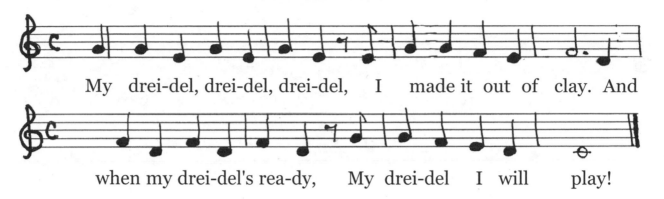

My drei-del, drei-del, drei-del, I made it out of clay. And

when my drei-del's rea-dy, My drei-del I will play!

Sing a Song of Winter

Sing a song of win - ter, frost is in the air.

Sing a song of win - ter, snow-flakes ev'ry - where.

Sing a song of win - ter, hear the sleigh bells chime.

Can you think of an - y-thing as nice as win-ter - time?

Fire Engine

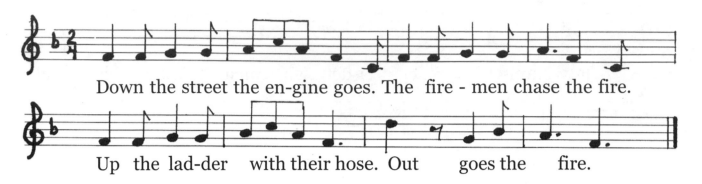

Down the street the en-gine goes. The fire - men chase the fire.

Up the lad-der with their hose. Out goes the fire.

Eensy-Weensy Spider

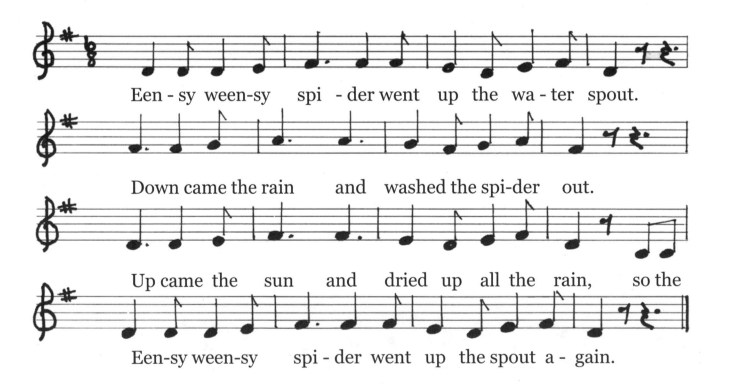

Een - sy ween-sy spi - der went up the wa - ter spout.

Down came the rain and washed the spi-der out.

Up came the sun and dried up all the rain, so the

Een-sy ween-sy spi - der went up the spout a - gain.

278

INDEX

ABOUT THE AUTHOR AND ILLUSTRATOR

Jill Dunford was born and raised in Salt Lake City, Utah. She received her BA in English education from the University of Utah. She has worked many years as a teacher and trainer in her church nursery and other programs. A former substitute Pre-K teacher and elementary school teacher in the Gwinnett School System, she has also taught seminars to other mothers on developing their own home nursery programs and stimulating creativity in children. She has been actively involved in PTA and the gifted program in her children's schools. She is presently a high school English teacher. The author of magazine articles on children, Jill currently resides in Grayson, Georgia.

Heather Dunford Nemelka, was born and raised in Dayton, Ohio, and Snellville, Georgia. A former Miss Teen of Georgia, she is a graduate of Brigham Young University in advertising. She has been employed in New York City by Simon and Schuster and Time Warner. Heather currently resides with her husband, John, and her son and daughters (second generation Teach Me Mommy students!) in Philadelphia, PA.

A PRESCHOOL LEARNING GUIDE

Teach Me Mommy,™a Preschool Learning Guide, is now in print again. This outstanding text was developed by Jill Dunford, the mother of seven children and preschool teacher and has been refined during twenty-five years of experience by working with educators and testing with other families. As a result, children who have been taught using **Teach Me Mommy™**enter school eager to learn and secure in their basic skills with an understanding of a world of knowledge.

SPECIAL FEATURES AND BENEFITS OF THIS NEW THIRD EDITION:

- nearly 300 pages of learning experiences give you plenty of fun subject matter – no boring reruns!
- 25 chapters with daily lesson plans save preparation time and do most of the work for you.
- hundreds of illustrations are provided – you don't need to be an artist.
- quick and easy recipes for treats mean you'll have more enjoyable learning experiences with your children.
- fingerplays and craft projects to help children "get into" the learning process.
- a "school year" format to coordinate with the schedules of school-age siblings.

PLUS WE'VE ADDED:

- an updated bibliography with the newest books.
- simple song melodies, so you can accompany your singing.
- an extended December holiday section including Hanukkah and Kwanzaa.
- an appendix with outlines for other holidays, including Mother's Day and Father's Day and recipes used in the book.
- updated day outlines, including dinosaurs and recycling.
- and information paragraph at the beginning of each unit indicating the skills the child will learn when studying the unit.
- easy to custom design with your own approach to spending quality time with your children.

SEE OUR WEB PAGE FOR MORE INFORMATION AND NEW PRODUCTS AT www.teachmemommy.com

- a book for full-size pattern pages with patterns for over 40 activities ready to copy or use as printed.
- A downloadable, electronic version that allows you to print out individual activities and lessons.

- CUT HERE - - - - - - - - - - - - - -

GLOUCESTER CRESCENT PUBLISHING
2175 HIGHPOINT RD., SUITE 104
SNELLVILLE, GA 30078
770.982.2277

Please send me _____ copies of **Teach Me Mommy**™at $24.95 (plus $5.00 shipping and handling)

Make checks payable to Gloucester Crescent. Allow four weeks for delivery.

Name _____

Address _____ City _____

State _____ Zip _____ Phone _____

Email address (for future publications and products) _____